THE ENCYCLOPEDIA OF
STITCHES

Edited by Karen Hemingway

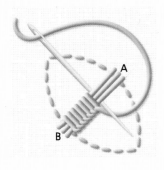
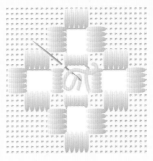

NEW HOLLAND

CONTENTS

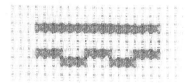
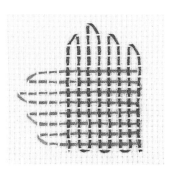
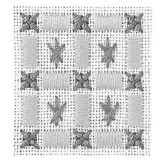

CUT WORK
101

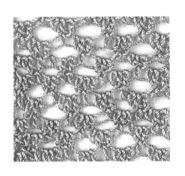

SMOCKING
139

CANVASWORK
149

GENERAL TECHNIQUES

Tempting as it may be to start stitching straightaway, it is well worth preparing and mounting the background fabric properly before you get down to work: time invested at the outset will always result in a professional finish. Almost all embroidery will benefit from being worked in a frame: the even tension prevents puckered fabric and distorted stitches, and you will quickly get used to sewing in this way. Protect your work in progress by pinning a clean handkerchief over the embroidery, then store the frame in a cotton pillowcase or wrap a larger piece with sheeting.

PREPARING THE FABRIC

When cutting out the background, add on a margin of at least 3 in (8 cm) all around the design area to allow for mounting. If necessary, wash and press linen or cotton, to prevent any later color run or shrinkage. Some cloth, and most canvas, will fray along the cut edges, so hem or zigzag loosely woven fabrics and bind canvas with masking tape.

Always mark the center of the fabric. Lightly press it in half length- and widthwise, then work a line of contrasting running stitch along each crease, following the weave carefully. This will assist accurate placement of the design and help establish a good tension when the fabric is mounted.

Silks, satin and lawns will need to be reinforced with a second layer of fabric to support the weight of the stitches. Cut a piece of muslin 3 in (8 cm) larger all around and baste the finer fabric centrally onto the backing, diagonally from corner to corner, across the center lines and around the edge. Where the embroidery is a small part of a larger piece for, say, a garment, trim away the surplus muslin, so that it only backs the embroidery.

MOUNTING THE FABRIC

Lightweight wooden hoops are portable and ideal for small scale work. To mount the cloth, loosen the screw and separate the two rings. The inner ring may be wrapped with bias or seam binding to protect the fabric and prevent it from slipping. Place the fabric over the inner ring and slip the outer ring in place. Stretch gently until it is taut like a drum, check that the guidelines are straight, then tighten the screw.

Using a scroll frame

Needlepoint and larger embroidery projects are worked on a scroll or "slate" frame. Hand-sew the top and bottom of the fabric to the webbing on the two roller bars. Adjust the bars to tighten the fabric, then secure the nuts. Lace the edges to the side bars with thick thread to keep the horizontal tension. For a long piece of work, the fabric will need to be rolled upwards as each section is completed and the sides re-laced.

Using a stretcher frame

These simple frames are made from four lengths of wood. Canvas should be cut to the same size and anchored to the top with thumbtacks: starting from the center top and bottom, then center sides, stretch it across the frame and work out towards the corners. Fabric can be wrapped over the edges and pinned to the back. To prevent snagging, the pins should be covered with masking tape.

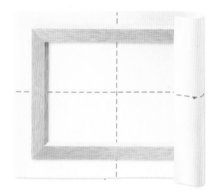

Fabric mounted on a stretcher frame

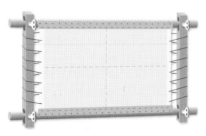

Canvas mounted on a scroll frame

WORKING ON EVENWEAVE FABRICS

Evenweave fabrics – linen, canvas and Aida cloth – are used for needlepoint, cross stitch and other techniques where the stitches need to be evenly spaced and of regular length. They are woven with the same number of threads in each direction to give an even grid across the surface. The thicker these threads, the greater the "count" or number of threads per inch (or 2.5 cm). This can vary from fine 24-count linen down to chunky 7-count canvas: high count fabrics necessitate small stitches in delicate threads, while the low count cloths require bolder stitches in thick thread.

Use a blunt needle and count the threads carefully to produce regular stitches. For horizontal stitches, count across the vertical threads; for upright stitches, count across the horizontal threads.

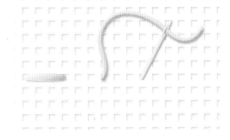

Working horizontal stitches on evenweave fabric

For diagonal stitches, count the intersections where the two sets of thread cross.

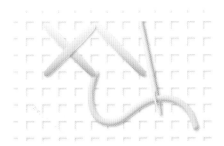

Working diagonal stitches on evenweave fabric

Following charts

Counted thread patterns are charted in colored squares or symbols across a fine grid, which resembles the mesh of evenweave fabric or canvas. Each square represents a single tent or cross stitch and the color or symbol corresponds to one of the thread shades. An identification key is given. Start stitching at the center of the design and work out. Make each stitch over the given number of threads or thread intersections.

TRANSFERRING THE DESIGN

Whether you follow a project or create your own pattern, the outline of a free embroidery design has to be transferred onto the background fabric. This can be done in various ways; the most appropriate method depends on the type of stitch, threads and fabric being used. Bear in mind that the outline must be accurate and that none of the marked lines should be visible on the completed embroidery. Enlarge or reduce the design to the size required using a photocopier. To make sure the design will be central, draw a horizontal and a vertical line to divide it into quarters and match these guidelines to the basted cross on the background fabric.

Tracing

Drawing straight onto the fabric is quick and straightforward. Sheer fabrics can be placed directly over the design, but for denser cloth a light box is necessary. This can be improvised by resting a sheet of glass on two stacks of books and setting up a lamp or flashlight in the space below. Tape the design to the glass, then secure the fabric over the paper. Alternatively the design and fabric can be taped onto a window or blank computer screen.

The outline can then be traced. On cotton or linen, this may be done with a sharp pencil if the stitches are not too delicate, but a water-soluble felt-tip pen will give a line that disappears completely. Always follow the manufacturer's directions and test a sample piece first: not all fabrics are suitable. Fading pens are useful for non-colorfast materials, but you may have to re-draw the lines (or sew very quickly!). A chalk pencil is ideal for simple outlines.

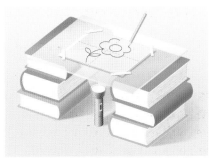

An improvised light box

Dressmaker's Carbon

This method is useful if a light box is not available. Use a light paper for dark fabrics and vice versa. Tape the fabric onto a flat surface, then place the paper face down over it. Tape the design on top, then trace over the outline with a ball-point pen. Brush any visible carbon away when the stitching is complete.

Hot Iron Transfer

Embroidery transfer pencils contain a heat-reactive permanent pigment, so remember that the outline will be indelible. If you iron lightly, the transfer can be used more than once, so this method is suitable for a repeat motif. Trace the design onto thin paper using an ordinary pencil. Turn the paper and draw over the pencil lines with the transfer pencil. Pin the paper face down onto the fabric (i.e. so that the side with the transfer pencil is against the fabric) and press with a cool iron. For a symmetrical shape, omit the first step and trace directly with the transfer pencil.

Tissue Basting

This method is used for transferring patterns onto dark or textured fabrics, such as velvet and satin, where a drawn line would not show up. It is also traditionally used for metallic thread work. Trace the outline onto tissue paper using a waterproof pen, then baste the paper to the the right side of the fabric. Using a contrasting thread, sew though both the paper and the fabric, following the lines carefully. Work in a neat running stitch and use smaller stitches over more detailed areas. When the design is finished, gently tear away the paper, leaving the design "drawn" in thread. Most of the sewing thread will be concealed with stitches: snip away any that is left exposed.

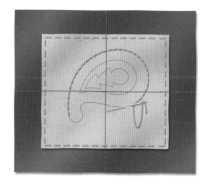

Stitching the design through the tissue paper and the fabric

Image Transfer

Advances in printing technology are creating exciting new ways to embroider. Iron-on image transfer paper can be used to put photographic images or drawings directly onto fabrics. Fine white needlepoint canvas, heavy cotton or linen all work well, although the process will stiffen the fabric slightly.

Blocking a Canvas

A piece of needlepoint which contains diagonal stitches will inevitably end up sloping at an angle, so restore its true shape by "blocking" the canvas. Dampen both sides with a water spray to moisten the canvas stiffener. Place a piece of plastic on a board, then pin down one corner of the canvas. Stretch diagonally and secure the opposite corner, then pull in the opposite direction and pin the other two corners. Use a set square and ruler to check that the sides are straight, then pin the edges to the board. Leave to dry away from any direct heat source.

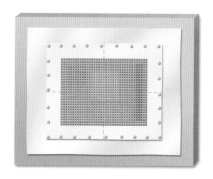

Blocking the canvas

Lacing over cardboard

Mount a project in this way before framing. Cut a piece of acid-free board to size and draw two lines to divide it into quarters. Trim the border around the embroidery to 1½ in (3 cm) larger than the board on each side and mark the center of each side. Lay the cardboard centrally on the wrong side of the fabric and pin the middle of one side to the board, placing the pin into the edge of the board. Pull and pin the opposite side. Check that the grain of the fabric is square to the board, then pin the fabric at regular intervals down the sides of the board. Starting from the center and using a strong thread, lace the edges together across the board. Fold, pin and lace the top and bottom in the same way.

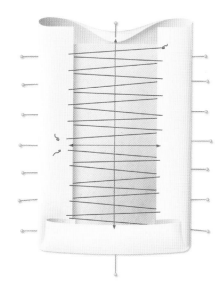

Lacing over cardboard

Mitering corners

Table linen and samplers are traditionally hemmed with mitered corners. Press under a double hem along each edge, then undo the second fold. Turn and press the corner so that the creases meet to form a square and clip off a triangle of fabric, ¼ in (5 mm) in from the diagonal crease. Refold the hem, then baste in place and stitch down. Slipstitch the miter.

The mitered corner ready for trimming

Counted Thread Work

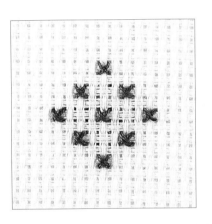
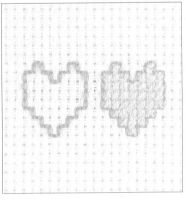
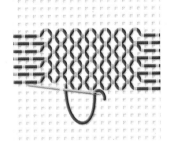

Cross Stitch

Cross stitch, or sampler stitch, is one of the simplest stitches an embroiderer can learn and yet, potentially, it is the most versatile. It can be used for working straight lines, motifs and intricate borders, and for filling solid shapes. Cross stitch has a long history and, until the advent of modern embroidered pictures, was used almost solely for creating intricate and beautiful samplers intended to display the embroiderer's stitching skills. Cross stitch samplers traditionally contained the letters of the alphabet, numbers, an assortment of figures and motifs, the year, and the name and age of the stitcher.

FABRICS

Cross stitch is always worked on an evenweave fabric – i.e. where the spaces between the warp (vertical) and weft (horizontal) threads are exactly the same – traditionally on linen, but nowadays often on a fabric called Aida. The fabrics can be loosely or tightly woven and are described by the number of threads to the inch/centimeter – called the count of the fabric. The stitches can be worked over one thread intersection (also called a block) for very detailed work or over two threads for less intricate patterns also making a square shape. Aida is available in a wide range of colors from white and cream through to darker shades such as navy and red. Linens tend to be available in natural and pastel shades.

THREADS

Modern cross stitch is worked using stranded embroidery floss. This is made up of six individual strands that can be separated and the appropriate number are used to suit the fabric count, so that the thread covers the background without looking gappy. For example, two strands of floss should be used for 14-count Aida. Stranded embroidery floss is available in a range of colors that stitchers of old could only have dreamed of. Fine pearl cotton, soft cotton embroidery threads and delicate metallic threads can also be used to add texture and depth to cross stitch designs.

NEEDLES

Use blunt-ended tapestry needles in a relatively small size to avoid enlarging the existing holes in the fabric.

USES

Cross stitch is not just limited to samplers and pictures, but can also be used to great effect on household linens and even clothing. There are a number of products available, such as tablecloths, that incorporate evenweave areas ready to be stitched. Aida is also available as a band complete with decorative edges in a variety of widths and colors. These are perfect for making edgings for dishtowels, guest towels, tablecloths and cushions.

Preparing the fabric

Cut a piece of your chosen evenweave fabric, allowing at least 2 in (5 cm) extra all around. Bind the edges of the fabric to prevent them from fraying (page 6).

Find the horizontal and vertical centers of the fabric and mark them both with a line of running stitches in a brightly colored sewing thread (page 6). Find the center of your cross stitch chart and mark this too with a pen.

Mount the fabric in an embroidery hoop ready to start stitching at the marked center point. Large pieces of work can be mounted in an embroidery frame (page 6).

Starting and finishing

To start an area of stitching, bring the needle up to the right side in the required square, leaving a short end on the wrong side of the work. Secure the end by working the first few stitches over it.

To finish an area of stitching and secure the thread, pass the needle back through a few stitches of the same color on the wrong side. Clip off all loose ends as you progress to prevent them from becoming caught up in subsequent stitches.

How to make cross stitches

Single Cross Stitch

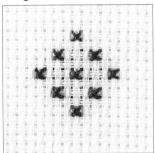

This is where an individual cross stitch is completed before commencing the next. Bring the needle up to the right side of the fabric in the bottom right corner of the square to be filled. Then take it down in the top left corner of the square to complete

the first part of the stitch. Now bring the needle up in the bottom left corner and take back down in the top right hand corner to complete the cross stitch.

Rows of Cross Stitch

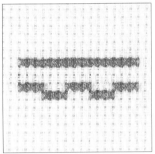

This is particularly suitable for filling shapes and for working simple borders. Working from right to left, bring the needle up to the right side in the bottom right corner of the first square and take it down in the top left corner of the square. Repeat

this first part to make a row of diagonal stitches from bottom right to top left of each square. Then return along the row from left to right, working each stitch from bottom left to top right to complete the cross stitches.

Half Cross Stitch

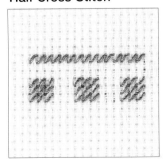

This is used for creating areas of shading. Although traditionally worked from right to left and from bottom right to top left, this stitch can be worked to slope in the opposite direction to catch the light in a different way. Work the stitches as for the first, or the second, part of basic cross stitch.

The following embroidery may also be used with cross stitch:
Beadwork (pages 50-53)
French knots (page 43)
Bullion knots (page 43)

Three-quarter Cross Stitch

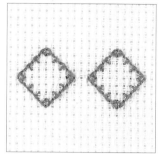

Part stitches are ideal for giving smoother outlines to shapes. Work the short part of the stitch first, from the required corner hole into the center of the square, parting the fine threads that make up the fabric. Then work the second, longer part as for the basic cross stitch.

Quarter Cross Stitch

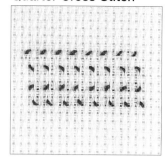

This is can be used as an open filling stitch, as well as to create smoother outlines. Work it in exactly the same way as the first part of a three-quarter cross stitch, always from one corner hole into the center of the square.

Back Stitch

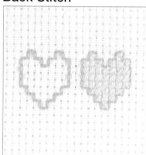

Back stitch adds definition to cross stitch figures and motifs, and therefore a more realistic appearance. It can be worked horizontally, vertically and diagonally, and over one or more blocks or threads. Working from right to left, bring the needle up one square to the right of the required starting point.

Take the needle back down into the hole at the starting point to make the first stitch. Bring the needle up again one square farther on and take it back down at the end of the first stitch. Continue in this backward and forward fashion to complete a continuous line of stitches.

Double Cross Stitch (also known as Leviathan Stitch and Smyrna Stitch)

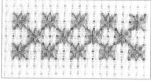

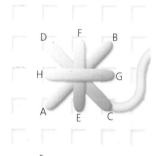

Although this is a canvas work stitch, it makes a very attractive cross stitch motif and can be used either to create interesting borders or on its own in the center of a square or diamond. It can be worked in two colors for decorative effect. Bring the needle up at A and work a large cross stitch over three horizontal and three vertical holes in the fabric. On top of this, work a large upright cross stitch in the sequence E, F, G, H. Bring the needle up again at C to repeat the stitch.

Assisi Work

In this type of work, cross stitch is stitched in the background areas and the motif or pattern areas are left unstitched. Assisi work is usually stitched in just one color and is best suited to dramatic designs made of simple shapes.

Cross stitch sampler chart

How to stitch the Cross Stitch Sampler

This charming and unusual cross stitch sampler has all the elements of a traditional design and will show off your skills to perfection.

You will need

12 x 15 in (31 x 38 cm) white
    14-count Aida fabric
Embroidery hoop or frame
DMC stranded embroidery floss,
    1 skein of each of the following
    colors:
Grass green (701)
Dark blue (796)
Sky blue (798)
Pale blue (809)
Mid-blue (825)
Purple (208)
Coral (351)
Lime green (470)
Mauve (554)
Pale pink (604)
Orange (741)
Yellow (743)
Deep pink (3687)
Tapestry needle
Two pieces of ¼ in (5 mm) diameter
    dowel, 12½ in (32 cm) long
20 in (50 cm) length of ½ in (13 mm)
    wide pink gingham ribbon
20 in (50 cm) length of ¼ in (5 mm)
    wide yellow ribbon

Key

✖ Dark blue 796
✖ Mid blue 825
✖ Sky blue 798
✖ Pale blue 809
✖ Coral 351
✖ Orange 741
✖ Yellow 743
✖ Deep pink 3687
✖ Pale pink 604
✖ Purple 208
✖ Mauve 554
✖ Grass green 701
✖ Lime green 470

Preparing the fabric and threads

1 Bind the edges and find the center of the fabric (page 6). Mark the center of the chart with a pen. Mount the fabric in the hoop or frame.

Stitching the center panel

1 Using two strands of the grass green embroidery cotton, first work the Assisi leaf panel in the center of the sampler.
2 Then use the four shades of the blue embroidery floss, with two strands each, to work the letters of the alphabet immediately above and below the Assisi panel.
3 Again using two strands of the appropriate colors, add the two narrow borders that separate the rows of letters.
4 Finally work the top and bottom rows of the alphabet.

Stitching the border

1 Using two strands of the coral thread, work the narrow alternating cross stitch border that frames the center panel.
2 Now add the border motifs in two strands of the appropriate colors, following the chart and key. Add backstitch with one strand of deep pink around the outlines of the small pale pink hearts in the top left corner.
3 Complete the stitching by working another alternating cross stitch border in two strands of coral thread.

Mounting the sampler

1 Place the sampler right side down on a clean towel, which will prevent the stitches from being flattened, and carefully press it on the wrong side.
2 Fold back the side edges eight squares outside the borders. Trim if necessary to make a double hem and slipstitch in place on the wrong side, along the border line of cross stitch.
3 Make casings for the dowels by turning back the top and bottom edges eighteen squares above and below the top and bottom borders. Turn under a hem, trimming if necessary and slipstitch in place along the border line of cross stitch on the wrong side.
4 Thread the dowels through the casings and hang with the ribbons.

Blackwork

A distinctive form of counted thread embroidery, blackwork was probably of Moorish origin and became popular in England during Tudor times due to the influence of Katharine of Aragon, Henry VIII's Spanish wife. As its name suggests, it is traditionally worked in black thread and can be embellished with touches of metal thread. Geometric patterns are built up by repeating stitch sequences within a defined area. The tonal contrasts you can create with blackwork give it great dramatic impact.

FABRICS
Evenweave linen or cotton fabrics are used for blackwork. The finer the weave of the fabric, the finer the finished embroidery will be, but take care not to choose a fabric that is so fine that the threads are too difficult to count. Plain white fabric provides the strongest contrast with the black thread and sets the stitch patterns off to good advantage, giving the technique its striking graphic quality. However, there is no reason why you shouldn't try off-white, beige or pastel shades of fabric.

THREADS
The type of thread you choose should match the weight of the fabric threads. For a crisp finish, it is best to use a single strand of thread. Pearl cotton, stranded embroidery floss, coton à broder and sewing thread are all suitable. As well as the classic black, other strong colors, such as red, can give an interesting effect. Fine synthetic metallic threads add richness to a design.

NEEDLES
Use a blunt-ended tapestry needle that won't split the fabric threads as you work.

USES
A sampler is an ideal showcase for the many fascinating stitch patterns you can create with blackwork. Set the stitch patterns inside geometric shapes or stylized floral forms for a traditional look. For a more experimental approach, try working a blackwork picture. Any design with large areas to be filled is appropriate, such as a house portrait, map, simple landscape of hills and fields, or city skyline with skyscrapers. Other items that are suitable for blackwork decoration include table linen, cushions and clothing.

Preparing the fabric
Cut a piece of your chosen evenweave fabric, allowing at least 2 in (5 cm) extra all around. Bind or overcast the edges of the fabric to prevent them from fraying (page 6).
Find the horizontal and vertical centers of the fabric and mark them both with a line of running stitches in a brightly colored sewing thread (page 6). Find the center of your chart and mark this too with a pen.
Mount the fabric in an embroidery hoop ready to start stitching at the marked center point (page 6).

Starting and finishing
To start an area of stitching, bring the needle up to the right side, leaving a short end on the wrong side of the work. Secure the end by working the first few stitches over it.
To finish, pass the needle back through a few stitches on the wrong side. Cut off all loose ends as you work to prevent them from becoming caught up in subsequent stitches.

How to make blackwork stitches and fillings

Holbein Stitch (also known as Double Running Stitch)

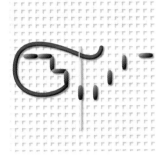

This stitch is used to build up a wide variety of blackwork stitch patterns and looks the

same on both the right and the wrong side of the fabric. It is worked in two stages. First work running stitch over the counted threads of the fabric, following the line of the pattern. Complete the stitch by working back along the same line, filling in the spaces with another row of running stitch.

Back Stitch (page 12)

Back stitch produces a similar linear effect to Holbein stitch and can be useful for certain blackwork patterns. However, Holbein stitch gives a smoother line and is less prone to distorting the fabric weave.

Flower Filling

Work each flower in Holbein stitch with an upright cross in the center. Build up the pattern row by row with flower shapes to fill the desired area. Then work the

small squares that link the flowers together. Finally, if you wish, add a border with a line of Holbein stitch.

Pineapple Filling

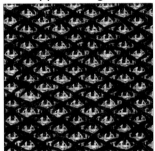 

Using Holbein stitch, start stitching the first row of the outline diamond pattern along the bottom of the area to be filled. Then work back along the row, filling in the

stitches to complete the diamonds, and add the groups of three straight stitches inside each diamond. Continue building up the diamond pattern row by row.

Honeycomb Filling

 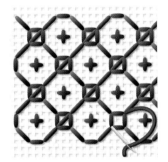

Using Holbein stitch, begin by working the lower part of the first row of octagons. On the return journey, complete the lower part of the octagons, adding the small linking squares. Continue in this way until the area is filled. Finish by working a

small cross in the center of each octagon and a short diagonal in each linking square.

Basketweave Filling

Work the first row by stitching groups of three vertical stitches followed by groups of three horizontal stitches, with each group occupying the same amount of space and a regular amount of space between each group. On the return

row, reverse the order of the vertical and horizontal stitches. Repeat as necessary. To complete the basketweave, add cross stitches to link the vertical and horizontal stitches.

Greek Key Filling

 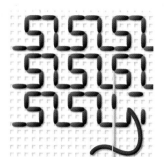

Use Holbein stitch to work the Greek key pattern row by row. The rows are separated by one fabric thread.

Square Grid Filling

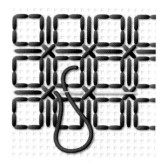

Work rows of small squares in Holbein stitch to fill the desired area, leaving two fabric threads between each square. Then add cross stitches to link the squares together. Complete the pattern by filling the spaces between the squares with long straight stitches.

How to Stitch the Blackwork Sampler

A pretty picture which demonstrates the different effects of six filling patterns within a geometric border.

You will need

12½ x 14 in (32 x 36 cm) 25-count white evenweave linen

Pins

Colored basting thread

Embroidery hoop

DMC coton perlé No. 8, 1 spool in black

Tapestry needle

7 x 8¾ in (17.5 x 22 cm) stiff white cardboard (or to fit your frame)

Picture frame (optional) or two curtain rings

The following embroidery may also be used with blackwork: Beadwork (pages 50-53), Cross stitch (pages 10-15), Coral stitch (page 44) and Chain stitch (page 39)

Key

All stitches worked in DMC coton perlé in black

Preparing the fabric

1 Bind the edges and find the center of the fabric (page 6).

2 Using pins and then basting thread, mark out six 1½ in (4 cm) squares, each 40 x 40 fabric threads, in two rows of three with six fabric threads between each square.

Stitching the sampler

1 Mount the fabric in an embroidery hoop.

2 Following the chart below, fill each square with the appropriate filling pattern. Take care not to pass long lengths of thread across the back of the work, as they will show through on the front.

3 To work the border, count 16 fabric threads out from the outer edges of the patterned squares to give the inner edges of the border. Mark this line with basting stitches.

4 Start at the center of one side, one thread up from the horizontal center line of basting, with a row of running stitch, working the corners with two stitches at right angles as shown in the border pattern diagram. Build up the border with three more rows of running stitch spaced two threads apart. Join the two center rows with straight stitches to make little squares. Join the remaining pairs of rows with cross stitches, working a three-quarter cross stitch at each corner of the border to give it an angled line.

Mounting the sampler

1 Remove all the basting threads. Press the embroidery with the right side down on a padded surface.

2 Place the sampler right side down and place the cardboard centrally on top of it. Lace the fabric over the edges of the board (page 8).

3 Place the mounted embroidery in a picture frame if you wish or sew two curtain rings to the back for hanging.

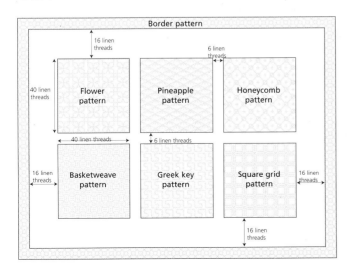

Border Pattern

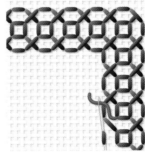

Corner detail of the border pattern for the sampler

Blackwork sampler chart. Enlarge on a photocopier for ease of working

Huck Weaving

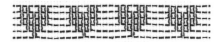

Huck, or Swedish, weaving is a simple form of pattern darning. A surface embroidery technique, huck weaving uses simple running and looped stitches that are worked under and over the floats on the surface of the fabric. The working thread is very rarely taken to the wrong side. Huck weaving designs are usually geometric and can take the form of repeat pattern borders or single motifs.

FABRICS

Huck weaving was traditionally worked on Huckaback linen, a towel fabric with very obvious floats (threads that lie on the surface of the weave), but it can be worked on any evenweave fabric such as Aida (which also has floats) or linen. The higher the fabric thread count, the finer the finished effect will be. A special fabric called Monk's cloth is also suitable and available in a wide variety of colors. It has eight squares to 1 in (2.5 cm) and has floats only on the right side of the fabric.

THREADS

Stranded floss and pearl cotton can both be used for huck weaving on Aida or Monk's cloth. On more openweave fabrics such as heavyweight linen or Binca, tapestry yarn can be used to great effect.

NEEDLES

Use blunt-ended tapestry needles that will pass easily under the floats without catching on them.

USES

Huck weaving can be used for a variety of household items such as tablecloths, napkins and throws. Worked on Aida band it can also be used to create pretty borders for towels, dishtowels and bookmarks.

Preparing the fabric

Bind the edges of the fabric to prevent them from fraying (see page 6).
Find the vertical center of the fabric and mark it with a line of running stitches in a brightly colored sewing thread (see page 6).
There is no need to mount the fabric in a hoop or frame.

Getting started

Most huck weaving patterns have quite obvious repeats and are worked in rows of stitches that start at the bottom and progress upwards. Center the design on the fabric using the marked center line. Always ensure that your thread will be long enough to work the whole pattern row, as it cannot be joined in the middle of a row.
Start the pattern in the center of the fabric, leaving a long length of thread, and work to the lefthand edge. Darn in the loose end. Return to the center point, repeat the design to the righthand edge and darn in the end. Any stitches at the edges that do not fit into the pattern can simply be worked in running stitch.

How to make Huck Weaving stitches

Running Stitch

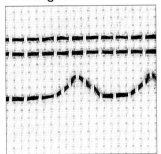

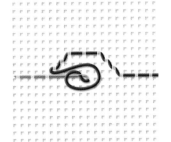

This is the most basic huck weaving stitch. It can be used to bridge the gaps between repeating motifs along a row or on the diagonal to create simple

zigzag patterns. Simply pass the needle in a straight line under the vertical floats of the fabric threads.

Offset Loops

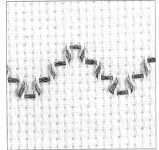

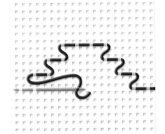

These can be used to create stepped geometric patterns. Pass the needle in a straight horizontal line under two floats. Make the next stitch in the same way, starting

with the float directly above the previous one. Continue in the same way to work up and down a stepped zigzag pattern.

Open Loops

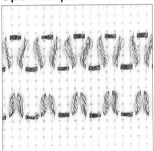

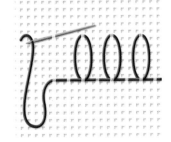

Open loops can be worked over any number of vertical and horizontal floats depending on the desired effect. For example, pass the needle in a straight horizontal line under two

floats. Make the next stitch in the same way, starting four floats directly above the previous one. Make the next stitch on the same level as the first. Continue in the same way.

Honeycomb

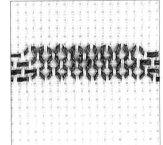

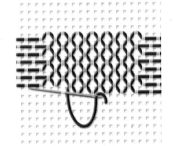

Work open loops through just one float in a diagonal pattern to produce the small zigzags. Offset the stitches on subsequent rows to produce a simple honeycomb pattern.

Closed Loops

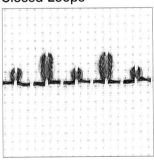

Closed loops, with one running stitch between each loop, make a very interesting simple border. Working from right to left, pass the needle through the float on the base line. Then pass it through the desired float directly above from left to

right. Finish the stitch by passing back through the base float from right to left and make a running stitch before starting the next loop.

Figure-Eight Stitch

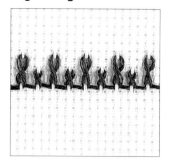 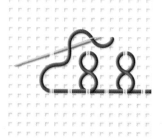

As its name implies this stitch forms a tight figure eight on the surface of the fabric. Work it in the same way as for closed loops, but pass the needle through the top float from right to left to create the cross.

Repeat motifs

Create simple repeat motifs by using a combination of closed loops or figure eight stitch. Join the motifs with running stitch.

Individual motifs

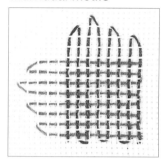

For individual motifs, bring the thread to the right side in the center of the square adjacent to the first float. Work the motif and then take the thread back to the wrong side at the end. Darn the loose ends into the wrong side of the fabric.

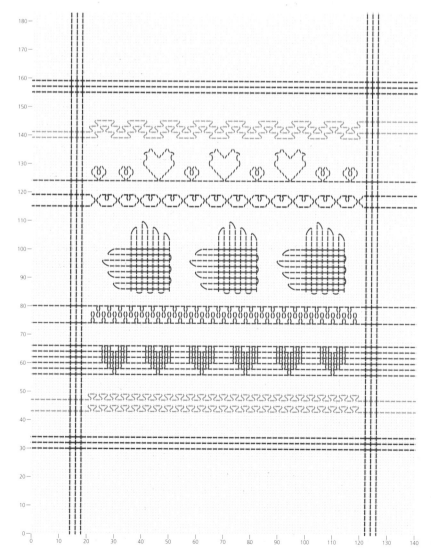

Huck weaving sampler chart: enlarge on a photocopier for ease of working

How to Stitch the Huck Weaving Sampler

Sweet and simple hearts in a variety of shapes and sizes give a Shaker-style charm to this little sampler. It is worked in four shades of blue, perfect for hanging in a country kitchen.

You will need

10 x 13 in (25 x 33 cm) white 14-count Aida fabric

DMC stranded embroidery floss, 1 skein of each of the following colors:

Dark blue (820)

Pale blue (809)

Sky blue (798)

Royal blue (797)

Tapestry needle

White sewing thread

Two pieces of ¼ in (5 mm) diameter dowel, 11 in (28 cm) long

½ yd (50 cm) length of ½ in (13 mm) blue gingham ribbon for hanging

Preparing the fabric

1 Bind the edges of the fabric and mark the vertical center line (page 6). There is no need to put the fabric in a frame or hoop.

Working the sampler

1 Use three strands of embroidery floss for the whole design and following the chart opposite. Work running stitch at the ends of every row so that thread can be started and finished outside the main stitching area.

2 Using dark blue thread and starting 30 squares up from the bottom edge of the fabric, work three rows of running stitch with one square of fabric between each row across the full width of the fabric. Work three similar rows of running stitch up one side of the fabric, 15 squares in from the edge. Count 103 squares across from that border and work another three similar rows of vertical running stitches up the opposite edge.

3 Leaving eight squares from the bottom border and using pale blue thread, work two rows of open loops. Work each loop over two horizontal and two vertical floats. Leave one square between each row.

4 Leave a space of six squares. Start the row of repeating heart motifs on the center line with sky blue thread, leaving enough to complete the second half of the row. Work one row of running stitch above the hearts.

5 Leave a space of seven squares. Work the next band of pattern in royal blue thread. Start the first row of figure-eight stitch one running stitch in from the vertical border. Work the second row of figure-eight stitches upside down to fit into the spaces left on the previous row.

6 Leave a space of five squares and then work the three heart motifs. Start the first heart seven squares in from the right-hand border and stitch it in pale and sky blue thread. Leave seven squares between each heart.

7 Leave a space of five squares. Using royal blue thread, work the first row of the next band in a pattern of three running stitches with two diagonal steps up and two diagonal steps down. Work the second row to match the first, but add a small closed loop stitch on the middle running stitch.

8 Leave a space of four squares and then work the running stitch heart border in sky blue thread.

9 Leave a space of three squares. Work the final band of pattern in offset loops using pale blue thread.

10 Leave a space of nine squares and then use dark blue thread to work three rows of horizontal running stitch, each row one square apart.

Making up the sampler

1 Fold back the side edges of the fabric four squares outside the borders, turn under a hem and slipstitch them in place on the wrong side.

2 Make casings for the wooden dowels by turning back the top and bottom edges 13 squares above and below the top and bottom borders. Turn under a hem and slipstitch the casings in place. Press the fabric carefully on the wrong side.

3 Thread the dowels through the casings and hang with the ribbon.

Free Embroidery

 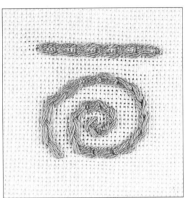

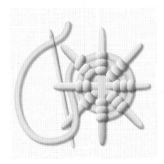

Free Embroidery

The stitches featured here are the foundations of free-style and counted thread embroidery traditions from around the world. They have evolved over centuries, each with its own particular purpose or decorative function, to provide a language of stitches that is constantly re-interpreted in different ways by succeeding generations.

Their names reflect this rich history - Pekinese stitch, Japanese darning and Russian cross stitch all echo their country of origin. Others describe their usage, such as blanket stitch, used to finish off woolen fabrics, or appearance, as the joined links of chain stitch testify. The natural world has provided names for ribbed spider's web, tulip, coral and sheaf filling stitches, as well as the quirky lazy daisy stitch.

Specialized types of embroidery have evolved that use just one stitch exclusively; for example, the intricate patterns of blackwork are formed with Holbein stitch and closed herringbone stitch is used for shadow work. However simple or complex they may appear, all stitches are formed in just one of four ways, and the following pages illustrate the various straight, crossed, looped and knotted constructions, each section starting with the simplest version.

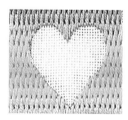

FABRICS

Almost any weight of fabric can be embroidered on from antique sheeting, muslin, or purpose-made evenweave to wool flannel, velvet, satin and transparent organza. The choice depends on the threads being used, the types of stitch, and the purpose and style of the finished piece.

The warp and weft of single and double-thread evenweaves form a regular mesh for guaranteed straight lines, while plain weaves such as linens, cottons, muslin and lawn allow for a freer style of embroidery that is not governed by the geometric weave of the fabric. Very fine fabrics that will not support the weight of the stitches can be backed with plain cotton (page 6). Fabric intended for household linen or making garments should be washed and pressed before use in case it shrinks.

THREADS

There is an inspiring selection of threads that can be used for free embroidery.

Stranded embroidery floss, which is mercerized to give it a sheen, is the most versatile: the six strands can easily be separated and used singly or in combination. By working with several strands of different colors, subtle blended effects can be created. Rayon floss is a brilliant synthetic thread that is also stranded. The single twisted thread of shiny pearl cotton adds texture to stitches, while coton à broder is smoother and gleams subtly. These two threads are available in skeins or balls in various weights. Flower thread is a fine matt thread, while soft embroidery thread is thicker and, unsurprisingly, soft. Silk thread is more expensive but produces glorious effects. The wool yarns intended for canvas work – tapestry, Persian and crewel threads – can all be used for free embroidery and especially for stitching on a wool background.

NEEDLES

Embroidery or crewel needles have a long eye, which will accommodate most threads: they come in different sizes and the length is a matter of personal preference. A fine tapestry or ballpoint needle, which has a blunt end, is used for evenweaves and is helpful for interlacing. A round-eyed quilting or between needle, which does not widen at the top, will slip easily through coiled threads for knotted stitches.

USES

In addition to creating pictures and samplers, free embroidery can be used to trim and decorate almost any personal or household item. Garments, including one-offs such as wedding dresses or baby robes, household linen and furnishing accessories, and any number of special keepsakes such as pincushions, greeting cards, bags or handkerchiefs can all be beautifully embellished with free embroidery.

STITCH FAMILIES

Although there are many very different free embroidery stitches, they can be classified according to their purpose and method of construction. They can be divided according to two main uses. Flexible outline stitches, in various widths, are used for narrow borders, outlining straight or curved shapes and lettering. Filling stitches are used to fill in motifs and background areas with individual scattered stitches, open patterns or solid color. Many outline stitches can also be worked in rows, spirals or concentric circles to make alternative fillings. Both types are made in one of four ways:

Straight stitches consist of single threads lying flat on the surface in lines, scattered singly or built up into geometric patterns or solid blocks. They can also be embellished by whipping, looping or weaving a contrasting thread over the foundation. They include crossed stitches, made by sewing one or more straight stitches over the first to make cross and star shapes or wide bands.

Looped stitches have two variations. Chained stitches are formed by making an oval loop of thread that starts and ends at the same point, which is anchored by the following stitch. These can be worked singly or continuously as border stitches. Buttonhole stitches are made by taking the needle over a loose straight stitch to anchor the thread, ready to create the next stitch.

Knotted stitches sit on the surface of the fabric like beads and are created by twisting the thread around the needle or an existing stitch. They should all be worked carefully as they are difficult to remove.

Isolated stitches often emulate shapes from nature. They make attractive accents used singly, but they can also make a scattered filling or be worked in rows.

Preparing the fabric

Cut a piece of your chosen fabric, allowing at least 2 in (5 cm) extra all around. Zigzag or baste the edges of the fabric under to prevent them from fraying (page 6). Mount the fabric in an embroidery hoop ready to start stitching (page 6). Always remove the hoop when you finish a stitching session to prevent the fabric from becoming marked. Large pieces of work can also be mounted on an embroidery frame (page 6).

Getting started

Stitches should be worked at an even tension and consistent length. For example, the links in a row of chain stitch should all be the same size, satin stitches should be the same distance apart and the slanted stitches of herringbone lie at an identical angle. Try practicing on evenweave linen to get the feel of sewing methodically, before working on plain weave fabric.

How to make straight stitches

Running Stitch

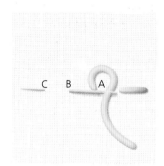

Use this stitch as an outline or a filling in straight or curved lines. Bring the needle up at A, insert it at B and bring it out again at C, to make the next stitch. Continue in this way, making stitches of regular length that are evenly spaced.

Cordonnet (also known as Whipped Running Stitch)

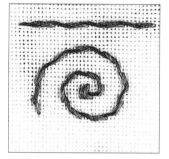

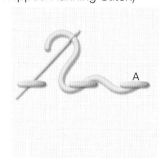

This stitch is particularly suitable for spirals and curved motifs. To whip a running stitch, thread a tapestry needle with contrasting thread. Bring the needle up at A under the first stitch. Then slip the needle down behind the second stitch. Continue whipping the running stitches in this way to the end of the line.

Holbein Stitch (also known as Chiara Stitch)

Made up of two rows of running stitches worked into the same holes, this stitch, taken from counted thread work, looks the same on both the right and the wrong side of the fabric. It is used especially for lines and fillings. Intricate patterns, in one or two colors, can be charted on graph paper. For the first journey, work every other stitch, like a running stitch, along the design. On the return, fill in the spaces between them, angling the needle slightly to create a smooth line.

Back Stitch (also known as Point de Sable)

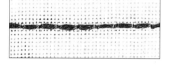

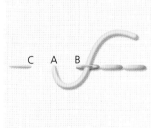

This can be worked in straight or curved lines. Bring the needle up at A and make a short back stitch to the right, inserting the needle at B. Bring the needle up at C, equidistant from A and insert it again at A to make another back stitch. Continue in this way, keeping all the stitches the same length.

Threaded Back Stitch

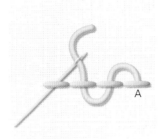

Plain back stitch can be embellished with interweaving in one or more contrasting colors. Using a tapestry needle, come up at A under the first back stitch. Slide the needle down under the second stitch and then up under the third. Repeat this weaving process to the end of the back-stitched row, then take the thread to the back to secure.

Pekinese Stitch (also known as Forbidden Stitch and Chinese Stitch)

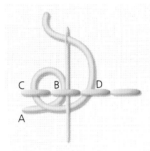

the second stitch at B and back down under the first stitch at C. Draw the thread through to make a loop. Now make the second loop in the same way, taking the needle up under the third stitch at D and back down under the second stitch at B with the needle on top of the loop being made. Repeat to the end of the back-stitched row.

For this more complex interlaced stitch, first work a foundation row of back stitch. Using a tapestry needle and now working from left to right, come up just below the first stitch at A. Slide the needle up under

The following type of embroidery may also be used with free embroidery: Beadwork (pages 50-53)

Stem Stitch (also known as Outline Stitch and Crewel Stitch)

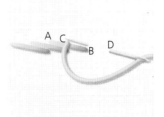

As its name suggests, this stitch is ideal for gentle curves such as stalks and tendrils. It is made up of overlapping straight stitches, which can be worked at a slight angle to the design line if a wider area needs to be covered. Working from left to right, bring the needle up at A and make a long stitch to B. Keeping the thread below the needle, bring the needle up at C, halfway along the first stitch.

Insert the needle at D to complete the second stitch. Keeping the thread below the needle, bring the needle up again just above B ready to make the next stitch. Repeat to the end, finishing off with a short stitch.

Split Stitch (also known as Kensington Outline Stitch)

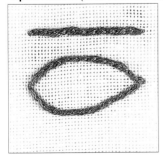

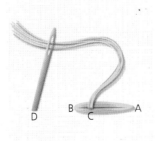

This stitch gives a smooth, flexible line that can be used for outlines, as the foundation for raised satin stitch and, in rows, as a filling. Use a sharp needle and an even number of strands of a loosely woven thread that can easily be divided – stranded floss or crewel wool is ideal. Start with a straight stitch from A to B. Bring the needle up through the first stitch, at C, and insert it again at D to complete the second stitch. Continue in the same way.

Couching (also known as Simple Laid Work)

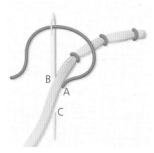

Corded, metallic and other threads that are too thick to stitch through the fabric can be anchored on top of the fabric with small stitches in a finer thread. This produces a bold, flexible line which can also be worked in rows as a filling. Bring both threads up at the start of the row. Using the fine thread, bring the needle up at A and then take it back down at B to make a stitch at right angles to the couched thread. Bring the needle up again at C ready to make the next stitch. Keep the tension even by holding the couched thread down with the tip of your thumb and make the couching stitches at equal intervals. Finish both threads off at the back of the fabric.

Satin Stitch (also known as Damask Stitch)

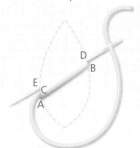

This filling gives a smooth, shiny surface. Starting at the widest point of the shape, stitch diagonally from A to B, then C to D placing the stitches close together. Continue upwards from E, varying the length as necessary. Bring the needle out again below A and work down in the same way to cover the remaining space.

Raised Satin Stitch

Work split stitch (page 29) around the outline of the shape to be filled to give extra depth to satin stitch. For a straight band, work the satin stitches at right angles to the outline. They should be so close together that no fabric is visible.

Overcasting (also known as Trailing Stitch)

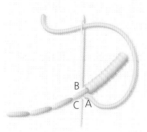

This cord-like stitch can be used whenever a strong, smooth outline is required and especially for stems, spirals and curves. In the 1800s it was used for monogramming linen. Make a row of split stitch (page 29) or back stitch (page 28) along the stitching line. Then work a line of small, closely-spaced satin stitches (above) at right angles across the foundation stitches, bringing the needle up at A and down at B. Bring the needle up again at C for the next stitch and repeat to the end.

Paris Stitch (also known as Pin Stitch)

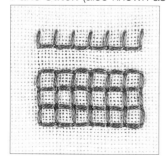

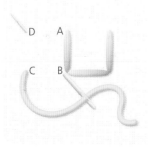

This linear stitch, which looks like blanket stitch (page 41), can be used as a border or in rows to produce a square grid filling. Keep the stitches equal in length for a regular look. Make an upright stitch from A down to B. Bring the needle up at C, level with B, and then re-insert it at B. Bring the needle out again above C, at D, level with A. Make the next straight stitch from D to C and repeat these two stitches to the end, finishing with an upright stitch.

Zigzag Stitch (also known as Triangle Stitch)

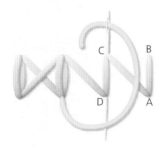

Work this stitch in two journeys, from right to left and then back again. Each

row is made up of alternating upright and sloping stitches, which together form a pattern of wide cross stitches. Vary the height and spacing of the uprights for a different look. Start with a straight vertical stitch from A up to B and then make a diagonal stitch from C back to A. Make the next vertical stitch from D to

C and repeat the combination to the end of the line, ending with an upright stitch. Working from left to right on the second journey and using the same holes, make the vertical stitches over the top of the previous ones and slope the diagonals in the opposite direction.

Backstitch Trellis

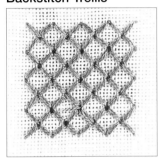

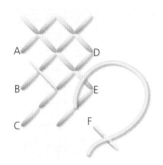

This geometric filling produces an open diamond grid, which can be light or dense depending on the thickness of the thread and the length of the stitches. Work a series of parallel diagonal rows of back stitch (page 28) from right to left,

starting with row A and working down, to row E. Then work the back stitches to complete the trellis, also in parallel diagonal rows, but at right angles to the first ones, starting with row D and working down to row F.

Japanese Darning

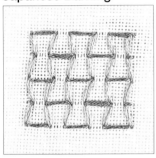

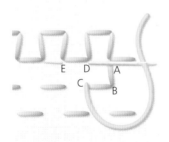

One of many beautiful Japanese filling stitches, this is traditionally worked in

white thread on indigo fabric. The foundation rows consist of running stitches (page 28) in which the spaces are slightly shorter than the stitches. Work the second and subsequent rows so that each stitch lies directly below a space. These horizontal rows of stitches are then joined with slightly sloping stitches. On the

second row, start with a pair of stitches from A to B and from C to D, then come out again at E for the next pair. Repeat to the end of this and the remaining rows.

Basket Filling

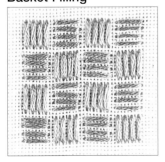

This interesting stitch gives an interwoven texture, useful where a representational effect is needed. It is formed from straight stitches, arranged in alternating horizontal and vertical blocks. Work on evenweave fabric and keep the stitches

regular. Begin the row with four parallel upright stitches, in the direction of A to B. The first stitches of the next block are worked in the direction of C to D. Repeat these two blocks to fill the required space.

Brick Stitch

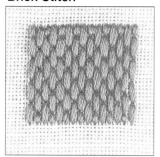

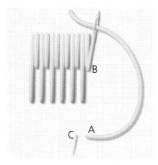

This solid or shaded filling is worked in interlocking rows of satin stitches. Starting at the left, work a row of alternating long and short straight stitches to give a straight line along the top edge. Start the second row with a stitch from A to B and bring the needle up again at C for the next stitch. Work all the stitches on this and subsequent rows of the same length and in the spaces between the stitches on the previous row. Continue working downwards and then finish with a final row of both long and short stitches.

Long and Short Stitch

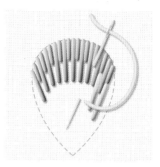

A more three-dimensional version of brick stitch (left), this shaded filling has traditionally been used to give subtle shading on petals and leaves. It looks best when worked in stranded floss, which gives a smooth surface. Work the first row in alternating long and short straight stitches, angling them towards the center of the motif. Fill in the next and subsequent rows with lines of straight stitch all the same length, each row in a progressively darker or lighter shade of thread and tapering off to a point.

Straight Stitch (also known as Spoke Stitch or Single Satin Stitch)

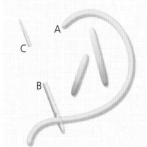

This basic straight stitch can be used in a free and graphic way or more formally to create flower heads and other design motifs. Overlapping rows of straight stitch, in different colors and lengths, are often used to represent grasses and for open textured fillings. To work, bring the needle up at A and go down at B. Come up at C ready to work the next stitch at a different angle. The stitches can be of varied lengths.

Seeding (also known as Speckling)

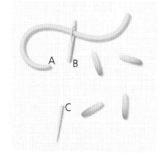

This filling consists of short back stitches, sprinkled at random. Bring the needle up at A and go down at B. Then start the next stitch at C. Keep all the stitches the same length.

Dot Stitch (also known as Rice Stitch)

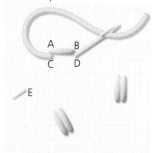

Where a more dense random effect is required, work short back stitches in pairs. Work the first stitch from A to B and the second directly below from C to D. Start the next pair at E.

Arrowhead Stitch (also known as Arrow Stitch)

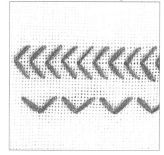

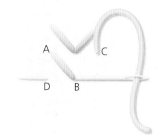

A simple v-shaped stitch, this can be used in rows as a border, singly as a filling or to make geometric patterns. Make a diagonal stitch from A down to B. Bring the needle up at C and insert it again at B to complete the

first "arrowhead". Start the next stitch directly below A, at D. Repeat the two diagonal stitches to the end for a vertical border or start the next stitch next to C for a horizontal row.

Back Stitched Star

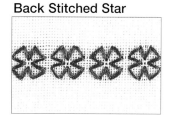

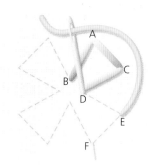

More of a cross than a star, this pretty stitch can be worked in rows, randomly or as an isolated stitch. Carefully follow the threads on an evenweave material to create a symmetrical shape. Work the top right arm first,

with three back stitches from A to B, C to A and D to C. The other three arms are worked in the same way, the second arm starting from E to D and F to E.

St George Cross Stitch

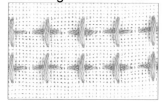

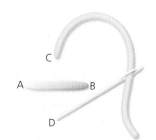

This is simply a basic cross stitch set "en pointe", which can be used as a random filing, in rows to form a geometric patterns or as an isolated accent stitch. Start with a horizontal stitch from A across to B. Bring the

needle up at C and insert it directly below at D to finish the cross. Always sew the horizontal before the upright stitch, especially when working in rows.

Ermine Stitch

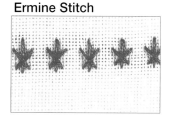

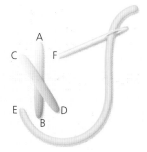

Resembling the heraldic symbol for ermine fur, this old filling stitch is often used in blackwork. It can also be worked in straight rows as a border or used singly. It consists of a long cross stitch set over a vertical straight

stitch. Work the upright stitch from A down to B, then make two symmetrically sloping stitches from C down to D and E up to F. The stitches should always be made in the same order.

Star Eyelet (also known as Algerian Eye Stitch)

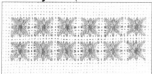

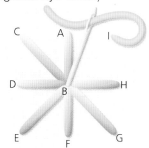

Also used in needlepoint and pulled fabric work, this square star is made up of eight straight stitches, all worked into a central point. This creates a small round hole, which gives the stitch a delicate, open appearance. Start with a stitch from A to

B. Then make seven more stitches into the same hole, working counterclockwise around the shape, ending with a stitch from I to B.

Square Boss Stitch

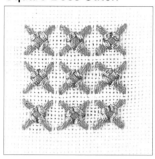

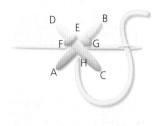

Work this raised stitch singly or in rows. The central square could be worked in a different color to vary the effect. Start with a cross stitch from A to B and C to D. Bring the needle out at E. Work a back stitch to F, then three further back stitches from G to E, H to G and F to H to complete the square.

Chevron Stitch

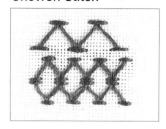

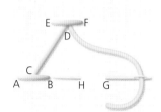

A zigzag border stitch, this can also be worked in rows to give a diamond lattice (known as surface honeycomb in smocking). It is worked horizontally with alternating diagonal and horizontal stitches. Start with a back stitch from A to B. Bring the needle up midway along this stitch, at C. Make a slanting stitch up to the right, to D. Then make a back stitch from E to F. Come out again at D and make the next slanting stitch down to G. Repeat these four stitches to continue, starting below F, at H.

Herringbone Stitch

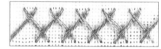

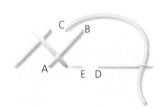

Threaded Herringbone Stitch

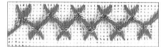

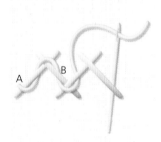

Work as a border or in rows as a diamond filling. Make a slanting stitch from A up to B. Bring the needle back up level with B, at C, and insert it at D. Come up again below B, at E. Continue by repeating these two crossed stitches.

Thread a tapestry needle with a contrasting thread to interlace a herringbone foundation. Come up at A and then slide the needle upwards under the first stitch. Then slide it downwards under the next stitch, at B. Continue to the end of the row.

Closed Herringbone (also known as Double Back Stitch)

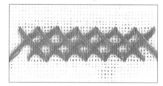

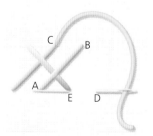

This is worked as for basic herringbone stitch, but without leaving any space between the pairs of crossed stitches. The stitch makes a pretty open border or a lattice filling when worked in adjacent rows. Make a diagonal stitch from A up to B. Bring the needle up to the left, at C. Make a slanting stitch down to D and come up again at E. Repeat these two stitches to the end of the row.

Fern Stitch

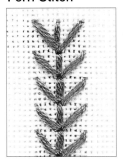

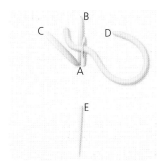

This pretty stitch can be worked geometrically, with all the stitches the same length, or freely to create more naturalistic foliage. It consists of three straight stitches which all radiate from the same point. Bring the needle up at A and make a straight stitch up to B. Then come up at C and work a diagonal stitch down to A. Complete with a stitch from D to A. Start the next group of stitches at E, directly below A.

Key

1 Star eyelet in gold 743 (4 strands)

2 Closed herringbone stitch in mid-green 3816 (4 strands)

3 Closed herringbone stitch in pink 602 (4 strands)

4 Arrowhead stitch in pink 602 (4 strands)

5 Japanese darning in pale blue 162 (4 strands)

6 Running stitch in salmon pink 892 (2 strands)

7 Whipped running stitch in mid-green 3816 and mauve 552 (3 strands each)

8 Threaded back stitch in mauve 552 (3 strands) and gold 743 (6 strands)

9 Back stitch in mauve 552 (3 strands)

10 Paris stitch in mid-green 3816 (3 strands)

11 Dot stitch in mauve 552 (3 strands)

12 Pekinese stitch in mauve 552 (3 strands) and gold 743 (6 strands)

13 Basket filling in pale green 3817 (4 strands)

14 Brick stitch in, from top: pale green 3817, antique green 3813, yellow 727, gold 743, yellow 727 and blue 162 (4 strands each)

15 Square boss stitch in salmon pink 892 and blue 162 (4 strands each)

16 Satin stitch in yellow 727 (3 strands)

17 Ermine stitch in salmon pink 892 (4 strands)

18 Back-stitched star in mauve 552 (4 strands)

19 Threaded herringbone stitch in salmon pink 892 and blue 162 (4 strands each)

20 Herringbone stitch in blue 162 (4 strands)

21 Zigzag stitch in coral 760 (4 strands)

22 Chevron stitch in pale mauve 554 (4 strands)

23 Couching in orange 741 (6 strands) and mauve 552 (2 strands)

24 Overcasting in salmon pink 892 (4 strands)

25 Stem stitch in mauve 552 (4 strands)

26 Back stitch in mid-green 3816 (4 strands)

27 Seeding in mid-green 3816, antique green 3813 and gold 743 (3 strands each)

28 Fern stitch in mid-green 3816 (4 strands)

29 Holbein stitch in, from top: gold 743, yellow 727, orange 741 (4 strands)

30 Straight stitch in, from left: pink 602, gold 743 and mauve 552 (4 strands)

31 Straight stitch in mid-green 3816 (4 strands)

32 Split stitch in mid green 3816 (4 strands)

33 Raised satin stitch in pale mauve 554 (3 strands)

34 Back stitch trellis in lavender 153 (4 strands)

35 St George cross stitch in gold 743 (3 strands)

36 Long and short stitch in mid-green 3816, antique green 3813, blue 162 (3 strands)

37 Back stitch in mid-green 3816 (4 strands)

Straight stitch sampler stitching chart: set photocopier to 111% to copy image to correct size for the embroidery

How to Stitch the Straight Stitch Sampler

This sampler introduces all the main straight stitches. It shows the fascinating variety and wide range of effects that can be produced by combining simple lines in different arrangements, lengths and colors.

You will need

16 in (40 cm) square of white 28-count
 evenweave linen
12 in (30 cm) embroidery hoop or frame
DMC stranded embroidery floss,
 1 skein of each of the following
 colors:
Lavender (153)
Blue (162)
Mauve (552)
Pale mauve (554)
Pink (602)
Yellow (727)
Orange (741)
Gold (743)
Coral (760)
Salmon pink (892)
Antique green (3813)
Mid-green (3816)
Pale green (3817)
Tapestry needle
Mat board to fit your frame
Picture frame

Preparing the fabric

1 Finish the edges of the fabric (page 6) and mount it in the hoop
or frame.

Stitching the sampler

1 Following the stitching chart on page 36, start by working the horizontal gridlines. Using two strands of the salmon pink embroidery floss, work two 5⅛ in (13 cm) lines of parallel running stitch horizontally across the center of the fabric. Then work a further pair of lines 1¾ in (4.6 cm) above and below.
2 Now work the vertical gridlines. First mark two points 1¾ in (4.6 cm) above and below the top and bottom horizontal lines and 1½ in (4 cm) in from the left end of the lines. Work two 7½ in (19 cm) vertical lines of parallel running stitches to join these points. Establish the second vertical line as before, but from the right, and complete the grid.
3 Embroider each section in the grid using the appropriate number of strands in the specified shades of embroidery cotton, following the stitch diagram and key. Where necessary, transfer the outlines (page 7) for the heart, letters and leaf shapes onto the fabric.
4 Work four star eyelets, one in the center of each side of the border. Then work the lines of closed herringbone, fern and arrowhead stitch. Finish the sampler by stitching another star eyelet in each corner.

Mounting the sampler

1 Take the completed embroidery from the frame and press it lightly from the back. Trim the surplus fabric to leave a 2½ in (6 cm) margin all around.
2 Cut a piece of mat board to fit your chosen picture frame and lace the fabric onto it (page 8). Place the mounted sampler in the frame.

How to make looped stitches

Chain Stitch (also known as Tambour)

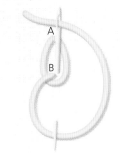

A flexible stitch, this is made up of a series of interlinked loops. It is useful for lettering and spirals as well as for outlines. Bring the needle up at A. Loop the thread from left to right and anchor it with a thumb. Insert the needle at A again and bring the point up at B, over the loop. Pull the thread through gently to make the first loop. Insert the needle at B again, inside the first loop, and repeat the sequence. Secure the final loop with a small straight stitch.

Open Chain Stitch (also known as Ladder Stitch and Square Chain Stitch)

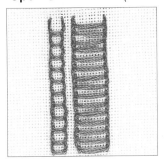

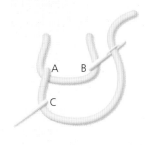

This can be varied by changing the width and height of the stitch, which explains the alternative names. Bring the needle up at A and take it down on the same level, at B, making a loop. Bring the point up at C, over the loop. Pull the thread through gently to make the first loop. Repeat the sequence to complete the line and anchor the last loop with a short stitch at each corner.

Feathered Chain Stitch

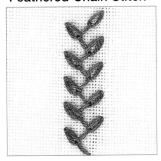

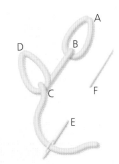

This stitch can be varied to change the angle and size of the stitches for a different look. Start with a slanting chain stitch from A to B. Bring the needle up at B and make a long stitch to C.

Come up at D to start the next chain stitch to C, slanting in the opposite direction. Make a long stitch from C to E and repeat the sequence from F to continue.

Cable Chain Stitch

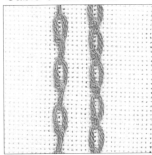

This interlinked chain takes a little practice, but can easily be mastered. Bring the needle up at A. Hold the thread down with a thumb to keep it taut. Pass the point of the needle under the thread from right to left, and then back over the thread to the right. Keeping the working thread under the needle, insert the needle at B and bring it up at C, again over the thread. Pull the loop up gently to form an interconnecting straight stitch and loop.

Wheat Ear Stitch

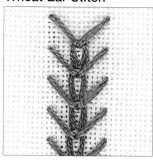

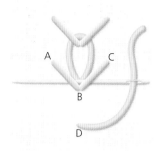

This naturalistic combination of straight and chain stitches is deceptively easy to work. Start with two diagonal stitches from A down to B and from C to B. Bring the needle up in a line below B, at D, and pass the needle behind the "v" of the previous two stitches. Insert the needle again at D to make a loop. Continue, alternating "v" shapes and chain stitches.

Detached Chain Stitch (also known as Lazy Daisy Stitch)

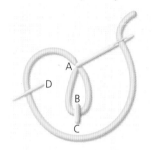

Detached chain stitches can be worked singly or in a circle to create attractive flowers. Bring the needle up at the center point, A, and take it down again in the same hole. Bring it up at B and loop the thread from left to right, holding it down with a thumb tip and pulling the thread gently through over the loop. Anchor the loop with a small straight stitch from B to C. Make the next stitch from A to D and continue clockwise to complete the flower.

Detached Wheat Ear Stitch (also known as Tete-de-boeuf Stitch and Oxhead Stitch)

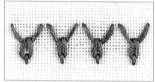

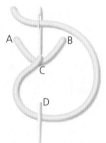

A combination of fly and detached chain stitches, this pretty filling is used in crewel work and as an isolated stitch. Make a loose stitch from A to B. Bring the needle up over the thread halfway between A and B, at C. Take the needle back down at C, holding a loop of thread with the thumb, and bring the point out directly below, at D and over the loop. Pull the thread through and draw up the loop to make a chain. Secure it with a small straight stitch.

Tulip Stitch

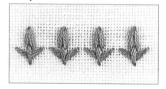

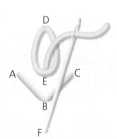

A pretty floral stitch, this can be worked in rows or singly. Vary the height and width, or use two colors, for a different look. Start by making an arrowhead stitch from A to B and C to B. Bring the needle up at D, directly above B, and loop the thread from left to right. Take the needle back down at D and bring it up at E. Pull the thread gently to form the loop to make the flower head and take the needle down at F, directly below E, to complete the stalk.

Blanket Stitch

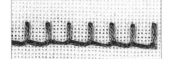

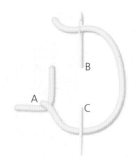

A useful linear stitch which can also be used to finish an edge. Bring the needle up at A. Take it down again at B and come up directly below,

at C, over the working thread. Repeat to continue, anchoring the final loop with a small straight stitch.

Buttonhole Stitch

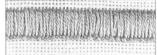

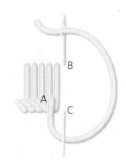

This is worked like blanket stitch, but with the stitches close together to cover the background fabric completely. Bring the needle up at A. Take it down again at B and come up directly

below, at C, over the working thread. Repeat to continue, anchoring the final loop with a small straight stitch. Keep all the stitches the same height.

Closed Buttonhole Stitch (also known as Vandyke Stitch)

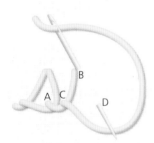

A triangular variation of blanket stitch, this forms geometric patterns when worked in rows. Make a diagonal stitch from A up to the right, at B. Loop the thread from left to right and bring the needle up level with A, at C. Insert the point

at B again and bring it out down to the right, at D. Pull the thread through over the loop. Repeat the sequence and secure the last loop with a small straight stitch.

Buttonhole Wheel (also known as Wheel Stitch)

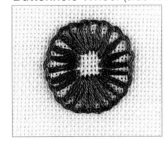

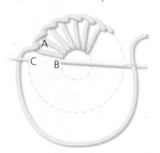

Blanket stitch can be worked within a ring to make a spoked wheel, ideal for flowers, eyes or as an isolated stitch. Keep the stitches closely spaced to prevent the outer threads curling inwards. Start by marking two circles on the

fabric. Bring the needle up at A on the outside edge. Take the needle down at B on the inner circle and bring it up, over the working thread at C. Continue stitching anti-clockwise, looping the final stitch under the first to complete the wheel.

Open Cretan Stitch (also known as Long-armed Feather Stitch)

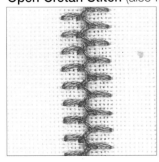

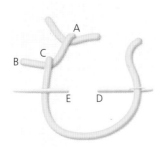

This spiky looped stitch is worked from top to bottom and can be used in rows as a filling. Make a loose diagonal stitch from A to B. Bring the needle up over the thread and level with B, at C. Make a loose diagonal stitch from C to D. Bring the needle up

over the thread and directly below A, at E. Repeat these two steps, stitching alternately to the right, then the left.

Fly Stitch (also known as Open Loop Stitch and Y Stitch)

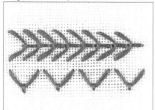

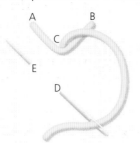

This adaptable stitch can be used as an isolated stitch, a scattered filling or a border. Start with a loose stitch from A across to B. Bring the needle out over the thread at C and take it back down at D to complete a single upright stitch. For a border, start the next loose stitch at E and the upright stitch at D.

Feather Stitch (also known as Briar Stitch and Plumage Stitch)

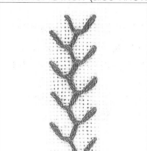

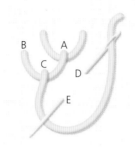

Traditionally used to decorate smocks and crazy patchwork, this is the basis of several other stitches. Like open Cretan stitch, it is a looped stitch worked from side to side. Bring the needle up at A and take it down to the left, at B. Bring the needle out over the thread at C and pull the thread through gently. Take the needle down to the right of C, at D, and then up again over the thread at E. Alternate these two stitches, ending with a short straight stitch.

Double Feather Stitch

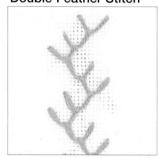

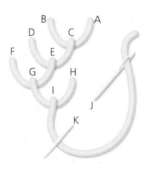

Work the first stitch from A to B. Then make two more stitches from C to D and from E to F in a similar way to feather stitch, but to the left. Bring the needle up at G and work two stitches down to the right. Carry on working downwards in the same pattern, alternating left and right. Finish with a small straight stitch.

Chained Feather Stitch

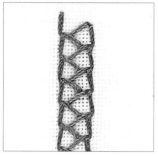

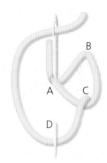

This heavier variation of feather stitch has an interlinked appearance. Bring the needle up at A and make a loose diagonal stitch up to B. Bring the point out over the thread at C, directly below B, and gently pull the thread through. Take the needle down again at A and come up at D over the looped thread. Insert the needle again at C to start the next stitch, then repeat this alternating pattern to the end. Finish with a small stitch to secure the loop.

How to make knotted stitches

French Knot (also known as Twisted Knot Stitch and Wound Stitch)

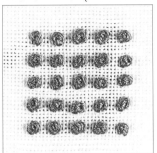

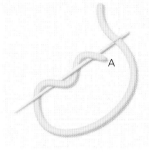

1 This round knot is extremely versatile. It can be used densely to represent flower centers, or singly to make eyes; it can also be worked geometrically. It

takes a little practice: the secret is to use a fine needle that passes easily through the loops of thread and to maintain the tension. Bring the needle up at A. Hold the working thread taut and, with the other hand, twist the point of the needle twice around the thread.

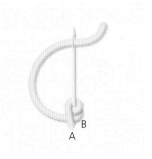

2 Take the needle back through the fabric at B, as close to A as possible, and pull the thread gently through, leaving a knot on the surface.

Bullion Knot (also known as Coil Stitch, Grub Stitch and Porto Rico Rose Stitch)

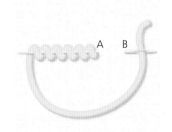

1 As for French knots, it is important to use a fine needle and maintain the

tension. Make a back stitch from A to B, the length of the finished knot, but do not pull the needle through. Bring just the point through at A and wrap the thread around it enough times to create the knot. Hold the coil lightly in place with a finger and pull the needle carefully through both the fabric and the thread.

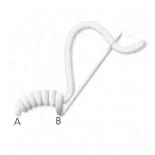

2 Take the needle back down again at B and pull on the thread until the loops lie flat.

Four-legged Knot

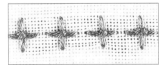

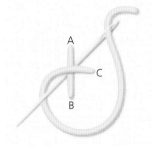

1 Resembling an upright cross stitch with a coral stitch at the center, this knot can be used on its own as an

accent stitch or in groups as a scattered filling. Start with an upright straight stitch from A down to B. Bring the needle up at C and pass it under the first stitch. Loop the working thread over the stitch to the left and pass the needle over it.

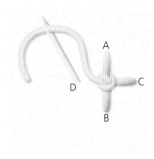

2 Gently pull up the thread to create a knot and take the needle back down at D to finish off.

Sorbello

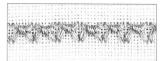

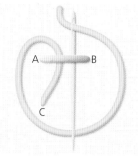

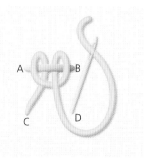

1 Work this Italian square knot in rows or as a filling. Work a straight stitch from A to B. Bring the needle up at C and pass it up under the first stitch. Holding the working thread to the left, slide the needle back down under the first stitch and over the working thread.

2 Gently pull the thread to form a knot and finish by taking the needle back down at D.

Coral Stitch (also known as Snail Trail)

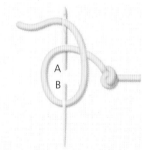

The alternative name of this linear stitch is wonderfully descriptive. The knots can be spaced closely or widely depending on the effect required. Insert the needle at A and loop the thread from left to right. Bring the needle up just below, at B, over the

looped thread. Pull the thread through to form a small knot. Start the next stitch a short distance to the left.

Pearl Stitch

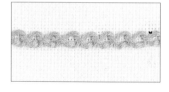

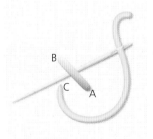

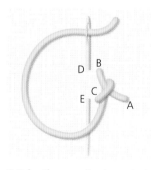

diagonal stitch from A up to B. Bring the needle up below B and level with A, at C. Slide the needle from right to left under the stitch and the loop, then gently pull the thread to form a small knot.

1 This gives a flexible knotted outline, resembling a string of beads. Make a short

2 Take the needle down just to the left of B at D to create the next diagonal stitch from C. Come up at E ready for the next knot.

Knotted Chain Stitch (also known as Link Stitch)

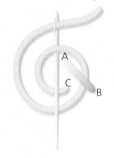

1 A heavily textured stitch that works best with thick threads, this is a cross between pearl and chain

stitches. Make a small angled stitch from A down to B and bring the needle up below A, at C. Slip the needle downwards under the angled stitch, then under the loop and over the working thread.

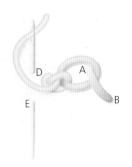

2 Pull the thread through to form a loose knot to the left of the straight stitch and continue working to the left.

Scroll Stitch (also known as Single Knotted Line Stitch)

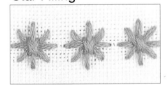

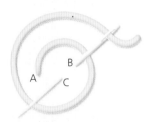

1 This knotted linear stitch is worked from left to right. Bring the needle up at A and make a stitch up to the right, to B. Bring the point out at C so that the needle is angled. Wrap the thread clockwise under both ends of the needle.

2 Pull the thread through carefully, maintaining the round loop. Insert the needle at D and come out at E, ready to wrap the next loop. Continue in this way to the end of the line.

How to make isolated stitches

Star Filling

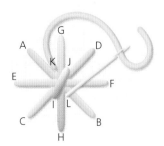

This round star is an effective isolated stitch, which can also be worked in rows or as a scattered filling. Work a diagonal cross stitch from A to B and then C to D, followed by a St George cross from E to F and G to H. Finish off with a small

elongated cross over the center, worked from I to J and K to L. This tiny cross can be worked in a different color to give a flower-like look to the stitch.

Ribbed Spider's Web (also known as Raised Spoke Stitch)

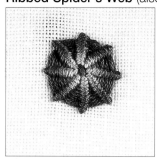

This is an attractive accent stitch. Start with a large star filling stitch (page 45) but omit the small cross on top. Thread a blunt needle with a long length of the second color and bring it up at the center of the star. Slide the needle to the left, under the first two stitches, then take it under the second and third stitches to make a back stitch. Continue until only the tips of the star can be seen beyond the raised ribs and finish the thread off at the back.

Sheaf Filling

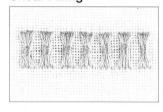
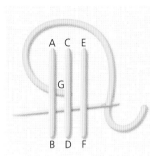

A traditional filling, which can also be used singly, this stitch resembles an old-fashioned bundle of wheat. Start by working three parallel upright stitches from A to B, C to D and E to F. Bring the needle out at G, behind the center of the second stitch, without piercing the thread. Slide the needle behind the stitches from right to left and take it back down at G. Draw the thread up carefully to pull the straight stitches together and finish off at the back.

Rose Stitch

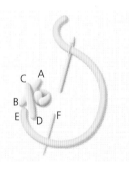

Use this for realistic flower effects and add detached chain stitch leaves or fine feather stitch foliage. The center is worked with a single French knot in the same or a contrasting color. The petals are then built up with rounds of straight stitches, worked in counterclockwise direction around the knot. Start with short stitches from A to B, C to D, E to F and increase the length progressively to complete the rose.

How to Stitch the Looped, Knotted and Isolated Stitch Sampler

This sampler makes a beautiful companion piece to the straight stitch sampler and introduces you to many new stitches. Spider's web and star, rose and sheaf fillings provide pretty accents, but all the stitches are fun to do and will give you a great sense of satisfaction.

You will need

16 in (40 cm) square white 28-count evenweave linen

12 in (30 cm) embroidery hoop or frame

DMC stranded embroidery floss, 1 skein of each of the following colors:

Shaded blue (121)
Lavender (153)
Pale turquoise (519)
Mauve (552)
Pink (602)
Leaf green (702)
Cerise (718)
Orange (741)
Pale gold (744)
Salmon pink (892)
Green (991)
Turquoise (995)
Pale turquoise (996)
Pale cerise (3607)
Dark sewing thread
Tapestry needle
Mat board to fit your frame
Picture frame

Preparing the fabric

1 Bind the edges of the fabric (page 6) and mount it in the hoop or frame.

Stitching the sampler

1 Following the stitching diagram opposite, start by basting a framed grid on the fabric to act as a guide for placing the stitches. Using dark sewing thread, stitch a 7½ in (19 cm) square outline in the center of the fabric. Then work a second square, ⅝ in (1.5 cm) inside the first line. Finally baste a grid of three horizontal and three vertical lines, approx 1½ in (4 cm) apart, to divide the inside square into sixteen sections.

2 Embroider each section in the grid using the appropriate number of strands in the specified shades of embroidery floss, following the stitch diagram opposite and key below. It may help to mark a ¾ in (2 cm) circle on the fabric as an outline for the buttonhole wheel and a letter "E" for the pearl stitch.

3 To finish the embroidery, stitch a star filling in each corner and then work the border so that the outside edge of each side touches the basted line.

Mounting the sampler

1 Take the completed embroidery from the frame and press it lightly from the back. Trim the surplus fabric to leave a 2½ in (6 cm) margin all around.

2 Cut a piece of mat board to fit your chosen picture frame and lace the fabric onto it (page 8). Place the mounted sampler in the frame.

Looped, knotted and isolated stitch sampler stitching diagram: set photocopier to 108% to copy image to correct size for the embroidery

Key

1 Star filling in orange 741 (6 strands)
2 Open Cretan stitch in pale cerise 3607 (4 strands)
3 Wheatear stitch in leaf green 702 (4 strands)
4 Detached chain stitch in turquoise 995 (3 strands)
5 Chain stitch in pale gold 744 (3 strands)
6 Bullion knots in lavender 153, pale turquoise 519, orange 741 and pale cerise 3607 (3 strands each)
7 Buttonhole stitch in lavender 153 (3 strands)
8 Double feather stitch in orange 741 (3 strands)
9 Coral stitch in mauve 552 (3 strands)

10 Four-legged knot stitch in pale turquoise 519 (3 strands)
11 Feathered chain stitch in leaf green 702 (4 strands)
12 Cable chain stitch in orange 741 (3 strands)
13 Spider's web in orange 741 (spokes) and shaded blue 121 (weaving) (4 strands each)
14 Detached chain stitch in green 991 (3 strands)
15 Rose stitch in pink 602, salmon pink 892 and cerise 718 (6 strands each)
16 Chained feather stitch in leaf green 702 (2 strands)
17 Pearl stitch in turquoise 995 (6 strands)
18 Tulip stitch in pale cerise 3607 and pale turquoise 996

(4 strands each)

19 Sheaf filling stitch in pale gold 774 and lavender 153 (4 strands each)

20 Open chain stitch in pale cerise 3607 (4 strands)

21 French knots in pale turquoise 996 (4 strands)

22 Detached wheatear stitch in mauve 552 (6 strands)

23 Knotted chain stitch in pale gold 744 (6 strands)

24 Sorbello in, from top: lavender 153, pale turquoise 519, cerise 718, lavender 153 and pale turquoise 519 (6 strands each)

25 Blanket stitch in mauve 552 (2 strands)

26 Detached chain stitch in green 991 (leaves) (4 strands) and pale cerise 3607 (flowers) (6 strands)

27 Fly stitch in lavender 153, pale gold 744 and pale turquoise 996 (3 strands each)

28 Closed buttonhole stitch in pale gold 741 (2 strands)

29 Buttonhole wheel in green 991 (4 strands)

30 Fly stitch in, from top: pale cerise 3607, pale gold 744 and pale turquoise 996 (3 strands each)

31 French knots in cerise 718 (4 strands)

32 Scroll stitch in pale gold 744 (6 strands)

33 Feather stitch in pale cerise 3607 (4 strands)

Beadwork

Beadwork has been used to adorn every type of dress and accessory, from Egyptian collars of lapis lazuli and Elizabeth I's jewel-encrusted gowns to Victorian bodices textured with jet and the dresses of the Jazz Age shimmering with beads. The Native Americans of the Northern Plains added bead embroidery to clothing, medicine bags and moccasins, and like the Kenyan Masai, their patterns and color combinations are symbolic as well as decorative. Embroidering with beads is straightforward: there are just four basic stitches, used to create a wide variety of effects.

FABRICS

Firm materials such as felt, velvet or heavy satins will complement the design and support the beadwork easily, but finer silks or cottons need to be backed with interfacing or voile to give the necessary extra weight. Single canvas is used for beaded tent stitch.

THREADS

Any thread that will pass through the hole of the bead can be used. Sewing thread or a single strand of embroidery floss is used for most work, but larger beads need a stronger thread such as quilting thread or special beading thread. A length of thread can be strengthened by running it over a piece of beeswax. Choose a color that closely matches the background fabric to make the stitch unobtrusive.

BEADS AND SEQUINS

Round seed or rocaille beads are the most commonly used and vary between 2 and 5 mm in diameter. They can be clear, opaque or frosted with square or round holes and with a contrasting or silvered lining.

Bugles, which come in various lengths, are cut from fine tubes of glass. This means the edges are sharp and can damage the thread. They are used when straight lines are needed within a design.
Sequins are punched from metal-effect plastic or fine sheet metal. Small sequins have a single hole in the center and larger ones, known as paillettes, have two or more holes around the edge.

NEEDLES

Special beading needles, which are especially fine and have a long eye, are good for couching beads, but they bend easily and can prove awkward for stitching. The finest size 12 quilting or embroidery needles will go through most sequins, rocaille and bugle beads.

USES

Beadwork is an effective way to embellish any garment or fashion or home accessory. Single accent beads will highlight subtle stitchery; bags or purses can be covered with beads and sequins; or beaded tent stitch can be worked with needlepoint stitches.

Getting started

The extra weight that beads add means that the background fabric should always be held under tension in a frame. An embroidery hoop is fine for smaller projects, but larger work should be mounted in a scroll or stretcher frame.
Knocking over the beads is an inevitable hazard. Avoid this by keeping them safely inside their original containers or in small jars and only take out a few at a time, as they are needed. Alternatively, put them onto a large plate lined with a piece of thick, dark fabric so that you can see them clearly. Thread the beads individually onto the needle by hand or pick them up on the point, directly from the plate.
Knot the thread securely when starting to stitch and finish off with a few invisible stitches on the wrong side. It is worth passing the needle twice through larger beads or when working seeded patterns to make the beads extra secure.

How to make beadwork stitches

Sewing Single Beads and Sequins

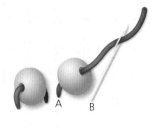  

1 To sew on a bead, bring the needle up at A and thread on the bead. Take the needle back down at B, far enough from A for the bead to lie flat on the fabric. Repeat as necessary.

2 To anchor a sequin with a bead, come up at A and thread on a sequin and then a bead. Take the needle back down through the hole in the sequin.

3 To sew on a sequin, bring the needle up at A and thread on the sequin. Take the needle back down at B so that the sequin lies flat.

Bead Satin Stitch (also known as Lazy Squaw Stitch)

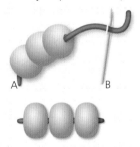

This can be used for stitching down short lines of beads. When they are close together, they give the appearance of bead weaving. Bring the needle up at A and thread on the beads. Take the needle back down at B, making sure the

beads lie flat on the fabric. Repeat this stitch to complete the rows of beads.

Bead Couching

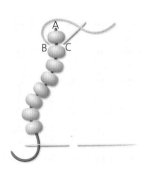

Longer lines of beads to make straight or curved outlines, are secured with a couching thread. Bring a beading needle up at A and thread on the required number of beads. Bring a fine embroidery needle up just below the top bead at B.

Make a short stitch across the beaded thread to C to hold the first bead in place. Continue couching in this way, following the pattern line and adding on more beads as required. Take both threads to the back and secure.

Beaded Tent Stitch

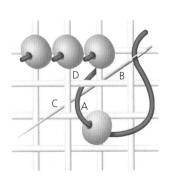

Beads can be stitched onto canvas on their own to form patterns or alongside needlepoint stitches. Bring the needle up at A. Thread on a bead and take the needle down at B so that the bead sits diagonally across the thread intersection.

Come up again at C, thread the next bead and complete the stitch at D. Continue adding more beads to complete the design.

Key
1 Flat silver sequins
2 Clear seed beads, size 11
3 Green seed beads, size 11
4 Lilac-lined seed
5 Lilac rocaille beads
6 Stranded embroidery floss in green, 704

Beaded pincushion design: set photocopier to 155% to copy image to correct size for embroidery

How to Stitch the Beaded Pincushion

Elaborate pincushions, swagged with glass beads and studded with sequins, were Victorian favorites and were often exchanged as love tokens. This contemporary version uses silver sequins and silver-lined seed beads to create a pattern of entwining leaves and hearts. As a gift for those who do not sew, it would make a jewelery cushion for a favorite brooch.

You will need

14 in (35 cm) square of fine linen
10 in (25 cm) embroidery hoop or frame
DMC stranded embroidery floss,
    1 skein of green (704)
40 flat silver sequins
80 silver-lined clear seed beads, size 11
360 silver-lined green seed beads,
    size 11
52 transparent lilac-lined seed, size 9
152 lilac rocaille beads
Beading needle
Embroidery needle
Matching sewing thread
7 in (17 cm) square of green cotton
    backing fabric
Toy stuffing

The following embroidery may also be used with beadwork:

Free embroidery (pages 26-49)

Stitching the design

1 Enlarge and transfer the outline of the design opposite onto the linen (page 7), indicating the positions of the sequins with dots. Mount the fabric in a frame (page 6).
2 Work the free embroidery, following the diagram opposite and key. Work the branches and tendrils in stem stitch (page 29), using six strands of thread.
3 Using the beading needle and referring to the diagram, attach the single sequins by anchoring each one with a single clear seed bead. Sew a circle of nine or ten lilac or green seed beads around the sequins, as indicated on the diagram.
4 Attach six sequins for the flower in each corner, sewing them down in a circle with straight stitches radiating from a center point. Add three lilac seed beads to the middle of each flower.
5 Outline the hearts with lilac rocaille beads, using bead couching stitch. Complete the hearts with an evenly spaced scattering of single clear seed beads inside each one.
6 Work the leaves in bead satin stitch using green seed beads, starting at the top and tapering the shape towards the point.

Making the pincushion

1 Remove the linen from the frame and trim it to 7 in (17 cm) square. With right sides together, pin and baste it to the backing fabric. Machine stitch a ½ in (1 cm) seam around the edges, leaving a 3 in (8 cm) gap in the center of one side. Clip the surplus fabric at the corners.
2 Turn the cushion cover right sides out and press lightly from the back if necessary.
3 Lightly fill the cushion cover with stuffing, using the point of a pencil to reach the corners. Do not overstuff it or the cushion will become distorted. Close the gap with slipstitch.

Shisha Work

Glittering shishadur, or mirror work, consists of small circles of mirrored glass attached to a background fabric with functional straight stitches, over which a round of decorative interlacing stitches is worked. The technique originated in India, Pakistan and Afghanistan where it was used both on clothing and within the home. Mirrors were often used in combination with bold, geometric embroidery, closed herringbone, chain and satin stitches, all worked in the brightest colors or golden threads onto vivid cloth. Shisha work is now being interpreted in new ways by contemporary embroiderers who have devised quick methods of incorporating mirrors and sequins into their designs.

FABRICS

Closely woven, medium to heavyweight fabrics, which are strong enough to support the mirrors and dense stitching, should be used. Linen, denim and cotton twill are ideal.

THREADS

Depending on the effect required, almost any strong thread can be used. Twisted pearl cotton produces a textured effect, while lustrous rayon, silk and cotton embroidery threads look especially good. If a stranded thread is used, be sure to work with all six strands. Metallic threads are often used in India and add their own reflective quality.

SHISHA MIRRORS

Real shisha is cut from handmade mirrored glass that has a grayish hue and is speckled with tiny air bubbles. It is flatter than machine-made glass and irregular in shape. As an alternative, metal spangles, large sequins or paillettes with holes near the edge can be used. Shisha ring stitch is an even quicker alternative: a small plastic blind or curtain ring is covered with buttonhole stitch and stitched down over a sequin.

NEEDLES

Use a sharp-pointed needle to stitch the mirror in place and a blunt-ended tapestry needle for the interlacing stitches to avoid splitting the thread.

USES

Shisha embroidery is traditionally used on clothing, hats, cushion covers, wall and door hangings and valances. On a smaller scale, individual mirrors work well as an accent, while bands or small motifs can be stitched onto furnishing accessories and bags.

Getting started

Always mount the fabric in an embroidery hoop or frame to maintain an even tension, especially when working with larger mirrors (page 6).
Use a small dab of fabric adhesive or a tiny strip of double-sided tape to secure the mirror before working the long stitches that hold it in place. Start and finish these stitches close to the mirror edge to make sure that it will not work loose.
Attach large sequins or metal disks with holes near the rim with sewing thread, which will be concealed by the decorative stitches.

How to make shisha stitches

Shisha Stitch

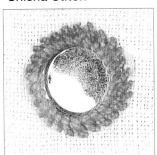

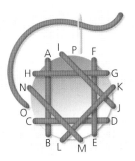

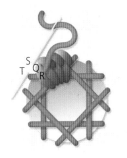

The following embroidery may also be used with shisha work:
Free embroidery (pages 26-49)

1 Secure the mirror to the fabric with eight long stitches, following the diagram and working clockwise from A to B, C to D etc. Take the needle down at P to complete the framework.

2 To work the decorative framework, come up Q and slide the needle under the stitches from the center outwards. Bring it out to the right of the working thread at R. Make a short stitch from R to S and come up at T.

Repeat until the mirror is completely surrounded by stitches.

Shisha Variation

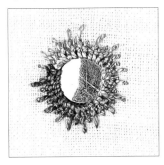

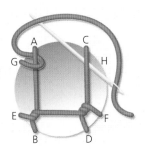

1 Work two long stitches from A to B and C to D. Come up at E and pass the needle under and over the first stitch, then under and over the second. Take the needle down at F. Starting at G, weave another stitch in the same way at the top.

2 To work the decorative stitches, bring the needle up at I and take it over and under the framework, coming out to the left of the working thread. Make a short stitch from J to K and pull the needle over the working thread. Take the

needle back over the framework and repeat the sequence to cover the framework, working alternate long and short stitches.

Shisha Ring

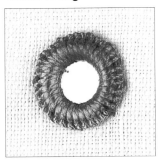

Thread a tapestry needle with a long length of thread. Hold the loose end against the ring so that it will be secured by the stitches. Bring the needle up through the center of the ring leaving a loop of thread to the left. Pass the needle over the

front of the ring and then from left to right through the loop. Pull the thread tightly. Repeat to cover the ring. Finish by passing the needle behind the stitches. Sew the ring onto the fabric over a sequin, using small stitches in matching sewing thread.

Shisha Grid

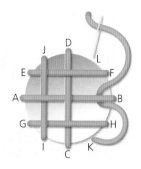

This new variation is quick and easy to work. Secure the mirror with a large cross stitch from A to B and C to D. Then work two evenly spaced stitches from E to F and G to H. Make two more stitches at right angles to the last two, from I to J and K to L, passing the needle under the central stitch from A to B to make a woven framework. Complete with chain stitches (see page 39) worked close around the edge of the mirror.

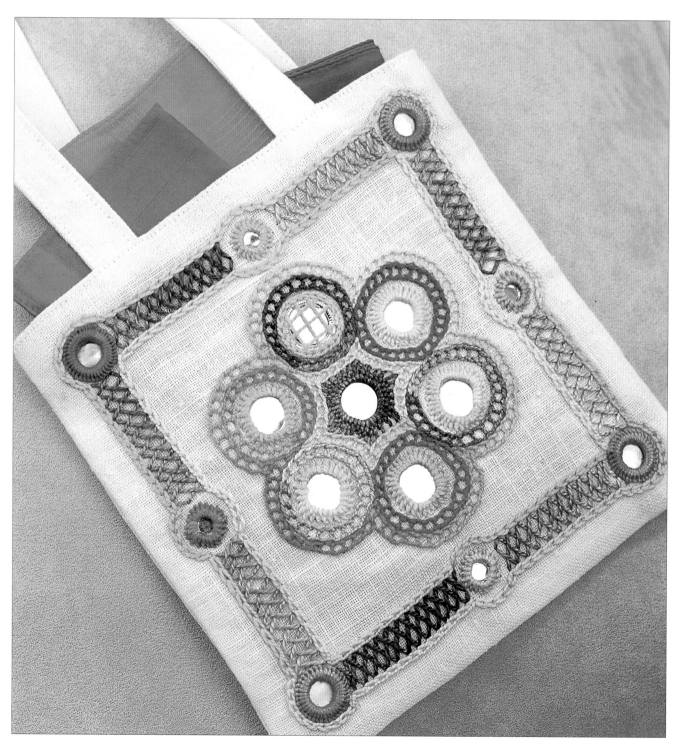

How to Stitch the Shisha Bag

The appeal of much shisha work lies in its characteristic irregularities, both in the glass itself and in the way the stitches have been worked. This design for a small bag was inspired by the richness and informality of antique embroideries. It incorporates some of the stitches traditionally used in India and the variegated pearl cotton adds depth to the colors.

You will need

12 x 16 in (30 x 40 cm) medium-weight
 linen
Dressmaker's pencil
20 in (50 cm) embroidery frame
Long-eyed embroidery needle
Fine tapestry needle
7 x ⅝ in (15 mm) and 8 x ⅜ in (10 mm)
 shisha mirrors or sequins
DMC coton perlé No. 5, 1 skein of each
 of the following colors:
Orange (51)
Yellow (90)
Purple (95)
Red (107)
2 x 7¼ in (18 cm) squares of cotton
 lining fabric
Matching sewing threads

Stitching the design

1 Enlarge and transfer the design outline below onto one end of the linen, leaving a margin of 2 in (5 cm) all around. Mount the linen on the frame (page 6).

2 Sew one of the larger mirrors down for each of the six petal shapes, following the diagram and key for the stitches and shades. Work the open chain stitch around each mirror as indicated.

3 Attach a larger mirror in the center and work shisha variation, so that the stitches fill the hexagonal space.

4 Sew the smaller mirrors and sequins to the border. Work the closed herringbone stitch around the rest of the border. Outline the inside and outside edges of the border with chain stitch.

Making the bag

1 Trim the embroidery to 7¼ in (18 cm) square, making sure the design is central. Cut a matching square of linen for the back of the bag.

2 Cut two 2⅜ x 12 in (6 x 30 cm) strips of linen for the handles. Press each strip in half lengthwise and the open the linen out. Turn over an allowance of ¼ in (0.75 cm) along each edge and press again. Re-fold each strip, baste along the long open edges, then topstitch along each long edge.

3 Pin and baste the handles in place 2 in (5 cm) in from each top corner on the linen for the front of the bag. Repeat for the back piece. Lining up the raw edges and with right sides together, pin and baste the linen for the back to the front of the bag. Machine stitch the front and back together, taking a ⅜ in (1 cm) seam around the sides and bottom edges.

4 Join the two pieces of lining in the same way, but leave a 3 in (8 cm) gap in the bottom seam. Clip the corners of both the bag and lining.

5 Slip the lining over the bag, right sides together. Pin and baste together around the top edge, aligning the side seams and with the handles between the two layers. Machine stitch around the top ⅜ in (1 cm) from the edge.

6 Pull the bag through the gap in the lining. Slipstitch the gap to close and ease the lining into place in the bag. Lightly press the top edge and top stitch around it close to the edge.

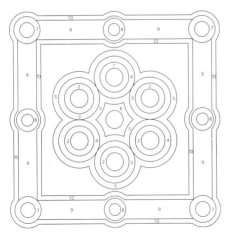

Shisha bag design: set photocopier to 250% to copy the design to the correct size for the embroidery

Key

1 Shisha grid in yellow 90
2 Shisha stitch in yellow 90
3 Open chain in red 107
4 Open chain in purple 95
5 Open chain in orange 51
6 Shisha variation in purple 95
7 Shisha ring in red 107
8 Shisha stitch in yellow 90
9 Closed herringbone in purple 95
10 Chain stitch in yellow 90

Crewel Work

✳✳✳✳✳✳✳

Any free embroidery worked in loosely spun wool is called crewel work or Jacobean work. It is easy and quick to work, and the variety of stitches offer great scope for individual interpretation. Its history can be traced back to the laid work used on the Bayeaux Tapestry, but crewel work reached its peak at the turn of the seventeenth century, when imaginative images of branching trees, flora and fauna were stitched onto bed hangings, workbags, cushions and even shoes. In Britain, the designs were heavily worked in dense color. However, in America the patterns became much lighter and more delicate because wool was scarce among the settlers and embroiderers opted for designs and stitches that used less yarn. Crewel embroidery was re-discovered by the Art Needlework Movement in the 1880s, chiefly by William Morris and his family. A second revival took place in the 1920s and 30s, when Jacobean work became a favorite way to decorate mock-Tudor homes and, in its various forms, crewel work retains its popularity today.

FABRICS
Crewel work is usually done on twill, with a diagonal weave, or on linen that is closely woven and firm without being too stiff. Unbleached or cream fabric, rather than a bright white, provides a complementary background for the muted colors of the yarn.

THREADS
Crewel wool is a lightly twisted two-ply yarn made from pure new wool, which has been used in the same form for six centuries. It is available in small skeins or larger hanks in a range of traditional and modern colors. Single strands of 3-ply Persian wool, which is slightly thicker, can also be used.

NEEDLES
Medium-length crewel needles are sharp-pointed and thick enough to pierce a hole through which the yarn can pass without damage. They have a long eye that can easily be threaded without fraying the yarn. Size 2 is used for Persian yarn or two strands of crewel wool and size 3 for working with a single 2-ply strand. Use a tapestry needle for threading and lacing composite stitches.

USES
Crewel work has been chosen for furnishing accessories and other household items for centuries. Few people would embark on a set of curtains or a large wall hanging today, but the motifs are versatile and are ideal for cushions, bags and glasses cases or for upholstering a special chair seat.

Getting started

Mount the fabric in an embroidery hoop or frame (page 6), depending on the size of the design, to maintain an even tension. A free-standing frame will keep both hands free for stitching.

Use one single or two strands of yarn, depending on the thickness of stitch required. Cut a length of not more than 13 in (35 cm): the yarn becomes slightly worn as it passes backwards and forwards through the fabric and the stitches can take on a frayed appearance if the yarn is too long.

Choosing colors and stitches: The natural dyes used on the original hand-spun yarns produced distinctive soft colors that are still used today – earth tones of terracotta, rose and ocher, along with soft hues of green and indigo. Traditional crewel work uses a restricted palette of closely related colors. Several shades of one color are often used within a single motif to produce the characteristic three-dimensional shading, which is usually worked in long and short stitch or parallel rows of chain or stem stitches. Two different shades of yarn can be threaded into the needle and used together for subtle color effects.

The illustrative nature of crewel work means that one type of stitch is used to outline the shapes and another type to fill them in. In addition to the open fillings in this section, many of the stitches from the free embroidery section can be used in crewel work. The stitches fall into three groups, each with a particular purpose in a design.

For outlining shapes and linear details: Choose back, buttonhole, chain, coral, feather, fern, herringbone, pearl, running, split and stem stitch, and couching.

For lightweight, scattered fillings: Choose arrowhead, bullion knot, detached chain, detached wheatear, dot, ermine, fly, straight, woven spider's web stitch, and French knots and seeding.

For solid fillings to give dense areas of color and shading: Choose brick filling, closed herringbone, long and short, and satin stitch.

How to make crewel work stitches

Jacobean Couching (also kown as Trellis Couching)

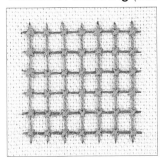

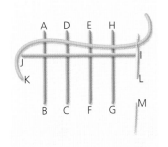

set at right angles across the first from I to J, K to L, etc.
2 Work small cross stitches, from N to O and Q to P, and repeat across the horizontal rows to tie down the points where the long stitches intersect.

1 Lay the foundation grid by working two sets of parallel lines across the area to be

filled. Start with long stitches from A to B, C to D, E to F, G to H, etc. Work the second

Battlement Couching

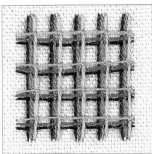

This is a development of Jacobean couching, which has a raised, textured effect. Lay down three grids of

stitches, each one positioned slightly above and to the right of the previous grid. Tie the top grid down, working small diagonal stitches from A to B, C to D, and so on in horizontal rows across the grid.

The following embroidery may also be used with crewel work:
Free embroidery (pages 26-49)

Honeycomb Filling

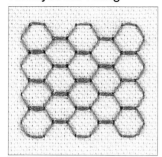

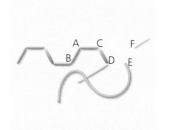

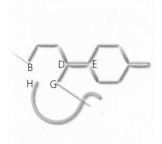

1 This open, hexagonal lattice is worked with two rows of stepped back stitch, sewn alternately forwards and backwards across the outline. Starting on the left, work four back stitches from A to B, C to A, D to C, E to D, etc, to the other side of the area to be filled.

2 Now work back across the area from right to left to make a mirror image with stitches from D to E, G to D, H to G, B to H, etc. Repeat these two rows until the required area is filled.

Cloud Filling (also known as Mexican Filling)

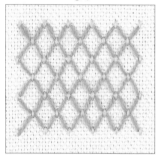

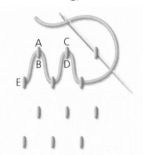

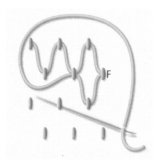

1 This interlaced filling is woven over a foundation of small, upright stitches. Work the first row of regularly spaced foundation stitches from A to B, C to D, etc, across the area to be filled. Work the second row in the same way, but with each stitch midway between the stitches above. With a second color, come up at E. Slide the needle under stitch AB, under the next stitch on the row below, under stitch CD and so on to the end of the row.

2 Start the next row at F and continue lacing in the same way, but in the opposite direction, to complete the row. Continue in the same way to lace through all the foundation stitches.

Double Cross Stitch

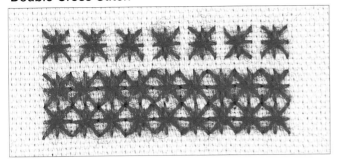

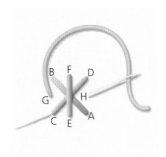

This dense filling consists of rows of square star stitches, which can be worked singly or close together in two

colors to produce a checkerboard effect. Starting at the top right of the area to be filled, make a diagonal cross from A to B and C to D. Then work an upright cross on top, from E to F and G to H. Come up at C again to start the next star to the left. Continue, working in horizontal rows to fill the required area.

Wave Filling

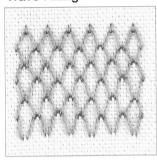

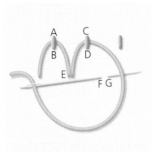

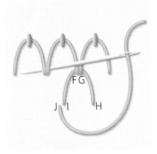

1 The tapered diamonds of this open filling are created by working horizontal rows of looped stitches. Start with a foundation row of short, regularly spaced upright stitches from A to B, C to D, etc, along the top edge of the area to be filled. To work the filling, bring the needle out at E and slide it under stitch CD. Then make a small horizontal stitch from F to G on the same line as E. Continue in this way to the end of the row.

2 Work the second row in the opposite direction. Come up at H and pass the needle under the tips of the stitches at F and G. Make a small horizontal stitch from I to J and continue to the end of the row. Repeat these two rows to fill the area.

How to Stitch the Crewel Work Cushion

This cushion cover is a reworking of Jacobean embroidery in contemporary colors. It was inspired by the exuberant work of generations of stitchers who paid little regard to scale or perspective as they incorporated a joyous mixture of bugs, flowers, vines, leaves and acorns into their lively designs.

You will need

40 x 20 in (100 x 50 cm) cream linen or
    cotton fabric
Embroidery frame
DMC Medici yarn, 1 skein of each of
    the following colors:
Pale yellow (8027)
Bright pink (8155)
Dark blue (8200)
Dark slate (8201)
Grey (8203)
Mid-blue (8207)
Brown (8306)
Beige (8322)
Tan (8324)
Apricot (8326)
Pale lime (8341)
Dark lime (8342)
Leaf green (8344)
Mid-green (8346)
Pale green (8369)
Dark green (8415)
Charcoal (8500)
Cerise (8685)
Pale blue (8800)
Orange (8941)
Tapestry needle
Size 3 crewel needle
Matching sewing thread
16 in (40 cm) square pillow form

Working the design

1 Cut an 18 in (45 cm) square of fabric. Enlarge and transfer the design on page 65 centrally onto it (page 7). Mount the fabric on the frame.
2 Work the design in single strands of yarn, following the stitch diagram and key on pages 64 and 65.

Making the cushion cover

1 Remove the completed embroidery from the frame and trim the fabric to 13 x 14¼ in (33 x 36 cm), leaving an equal margin all around the stitching. Press lightly from the back.
2 Cut a second piece of fabric the same size. With right sides together, pin and baste the two pieces together. Machine stitch a seam all around, ⅝ in (1.5 cm) from the edges, leaving a 10 in (25 cm) gap at the center of the bottom edge.
3 Press back the seam allowance along the opening. Trim the corners of the fabric and turn the cover right side out.
4 Ease out the corners of the cover and press the seams lightly. Insert the pillow form and then slipstitch the opening to close.
5 Make four 20 in (50 cm) plaits from the remaining crewel wool and slipstitch one securely along each edge of the cushion. Knot them together where they meet at the corners. Then trim the resulting tassels to 3 in (8 cm) and comb the threads out.

Key

1 Chain stitch in brown 8306
2 Honeycomb filling in tan 8324
3 Split stitch in dark slate 8201
4 Seeding in leaf green 8344
5 Seeding in dark lime 8342
6 Coral stitch in grey 8203
7 Bullion knots in orange 8941
8 French knots in brown 8306
9 Stem stitch in dark slate 8201
10 Raised satin stitch in pale lime 8341
11 Long and short stitch in apricot 8326, beige 8322, tan 8324 (from the top)
12 Jacobean couching in brown 8306 (laid thread) and dark green 8415 (crosses)
13 Buttonhole stitch in pale blue 8800
14 Stem stitch in charcoal 8500
15 French knots in charcoal 8500
16 Satin stitch in charcoal 8500 and pale yellow 8027
17 Straight stitch in charcoal 8500
18 Chain stitch in charcoal 8500
19 Battlement couching in brown 8306, tan 8324, apricot 8326 (laid thread) and pale lime 8341 (ties)
20 Long and short stitch in pale yellow 8027, orange 8941, beige 8322 (from the top)
21 Chain stitch in cerise 8685
22 Detached chain stitch in cerise 8685
23 Satin stitch in orange 8941
24 Satin stitch in pale yellow 8027
25 Chain stitch in dark slate 8201
26 French knots in mid-blue 8207 and mid-green 8346

27 Double cross stitch in bright pink 8155
28 Fly stitch in grey 8203
29 Long and short stitch in apricot 8326
30 Stem stitch in apricot 8326
31 Cloud filling in dark lime 8342
32 Long and short stitch in tan 8324
33 Stem stitch in tan 8324
34 Herringbone stitch in pale green 8369
35 Coral stitch in dark green 8415
36 Coral stitch in dark slate 8201
37 Buttonhole stitch in dark slate 8201
38 Running stitch in dark slate 8201
39 Chain stitch in dark lime 8342 and pale green 8369
40 Satin stitch in cerise 8685
41 Chain stitch in cerise 8685
42 Fly stitch in mid-green 8346
43 Chain stitch in pink 8155
44 Cloud filling in pale yellow 8027 (ties) and orange 8941 (lacing)
45 Detached wheatear stitch in pink 8155
46 Chain stitch in dark blue 8200
47 Seeding in cerise 8685
48 Straight stitch in pale yellow 8027 and brown 8306
49 Back stitch in cerise 8685
50 Jacobean couching in tan 8324 (laid thread) and orange 8941 (crosses)
51 Detached fly stitch in mid-slate 8302 and dark lime 8342
52 Satin stitch in pink 8155 and pale lime 8341
53 French knots and stem stitch in tan 8324
54 Herringbone stitch in dark lime 8342

Crewel work cushion design: set photocopier to 154% to copy image to correct size for the embroidery

Silk Ribbon Embroidery

Embroidery with stitches in fine silk ribbon instead of thread has been used to decorate fashionable garments from eighteenth-century French court dress to Victorian ballgowns and 1920's satin petticoats. In more recent years, however, it has evolved into an independent branch of needlecraft. Aware of its increase in popularity in Australia, the US and Europe, manufacturers are now producing a wonderful selection of soft silk ribbons that are specially designed for embroidery. The range of hues and shades available is inspiring and even a beginner will find that it is satisfyingly quick and easy to produce beautiful work.

FABRICS

Ribbons can be sewn onto almost any firmly woven fabric, depending on the effect required and the scale of the work. Velvet, silk dupion or taffeta will complement the ribbon while cotton muslin or linen will provide a contrasting texture. Back fine fabrics with voile to support the stitches (page 6).

RIBBONS AND THREADS

Silk embroidery ribbon has a loose weave, which makes it easy to stitch. It comes in various widths from 1/16 in (2 mm) up to 1⅜ in (3 cm), ⅛ in (4 mm) being the most popular. Ribbons come in a selection of colors from bright primaries and muted pastels to subtly shaded ombré. Double-faced satin ribbon can also be used, but it is stiffer and less easy to work. You will also need some matching sewing threads to secure the ribbon and stranded embroidery floss for any free embroidery stitches in the design.

NEEDLES

Choose a chenille needle with a sharp point and a long, easily threaded eye, which is thick enough to pierce a hole in the fabric through which the ribbon can slip without becoming damaged. A size 18 should be suitable for most work.

USES

Ribbon embroidery is ideal for small projects such as greeting cards and box-framed pictures. It can be also used to embellish evening bags, children's garments and baby clothes or lingerie and night wear. If the items need to be laundered, check that the ribbon is colorfast.

Getting started

Mount the fabric in an embroidery hoop or frame (page 6) that is large enough to accommodate the whole design without it being moved, in order to prevent the ribbon stitches from becoming crushed. Use a free-standing frame if possible so that both hands are free to manipulate and smooth the ribbons while stitching.

Working with ribbons: Silk embroidery ribbons are both delicate and expensive, so handle and use them with special care. Most are supplied on small cards which can be stored in a flat box, but any ribbons that are bought by length can be wound onto squares of cardboard to prevent them from tangling. Lightly press the ribbon with a cool iron before using it to remove any creases.

Locking the ribbon: Ribbon can become worn and frayed at the edges as it passes through the fabric, so only work with short lengths of no more than 12 in (30 cm). To maximize the amount of ribbon that can be stitched, a special technique is used to fix the ribbon into the needle without a long tail. Thread the needle as usual and then insert the point into the ribbon ³⁄₁₆ in (5 mm) from the short end. Gently pull the long end so that the ribbon becomes locked around the eye of the needle.

Starting and finishing

To start sewing, knot the end of the ribbon or draw the ribbon through the fabric so that a ⅜ in (1 cm) tail is left on the wrong side. When the needle is passed back through, hold this tail in line with the first stitch so that the point pierces and anchors it in place.

Finish off on the back by slipstitching the end of each length of ribbon to the back of the previous stitch using sewing thread.

Stitching with ribbon: Sew slowly and carefully, keeping the tension loose and shaping each stitch individually. The ribbon will twist back on itself as it is worked: this can be used to good effect to make narrow stitches, but when a flat stitch is required, hold it down with a fingertip or second needle as it is pulled through to the right side.

Choosing stitches: Silk ribbon is not suitable for fine details, which are usually added with stranded floss or pearl cotton. A range of stitches, including fly, feather, stem, straight, back and fern can be adapted to create stamens, light foliage, stalks and highlights. In addition to the stitches illustrated here, free embroidery stitches such as detached chain, straight, French and bullion knots can all be worked in ribbon and often the appearance is quite different.

Inserting the point of the needle into ribbon end

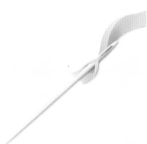

Pulling up the thread to lock it onto the needle

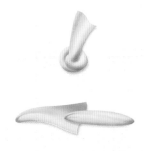
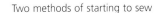

Two methods of starting to sew

Securing the ribbon end

The following embroidery may also be used with silk ribbon embroidery:

Free embroidery (pages 26-49)

How to make ribbon embroidery stitches

Ribbon Stitch

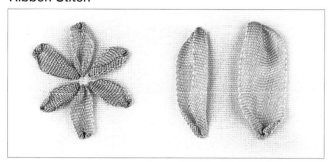

This stitch is ideal for flowers and leaves. Bring the ribbon up at A and smooth it along the fabric. Hold it down lightly at C and take the needle down in the center, at B. Slowly pull the ribbon through so that it turns back on itself.

Side Ribbon Stitch

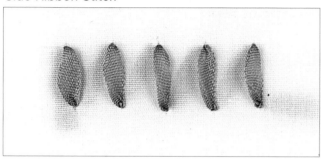

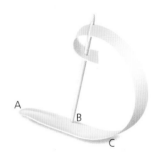

In this variation the petal turns to one side or the other, giving a flatter stitch than ribbon stitch. Work in the same way as for ribbon stitch, but take the needle down close to one edge of the ribbon, at B.

Back-to-back Ribbon Stitch

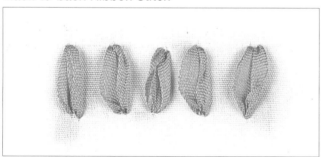

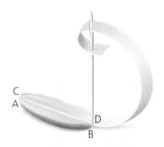

at D, to form the second stitch of the same length that sits close to the first. For a more pointed stitch, make two side ribbon stitches, with the left one pierced on the right side and the right one pieced on the left side of the ribbon.

Ideal for buds and leaves, this stitch comprises two adjacent side ribbon stitches. Work the first stitch from A to B. Bring the ribbon up again very close to A, at C. Take the needle down near the left edge of the ribbon,

Twisted Chain Stitch

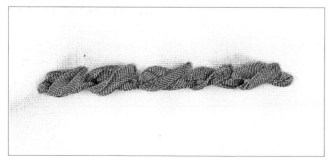

ribbon through gently until the loop is the size required. Bring the ribbon up at C and pull it through over the loop, allowing it to twist back on itself. Start the next stitch at C, looping the ribbon as before, inserting the needle at D and bringing the ribbon up at E. Repeat this sequence to form a chain of twisted loops.

This stitch gives a heavy, flexible outline. Bring the ribbon up at A and loop it from left to right. Take it back down to the left and slightly down from A, at B. Pull the

Loop Stitch

This open loop can be worked singly or in a circle to make a flower shape. Bring the ribbon up at A and place a tapestry needle or knitting needle, depending on the size of loop required, on the ribbon. Keeping the ribbon straight, take the needle down through the ribbon close to A, at B. Draw the ribbon through around the support and then gently pull out the support. Hold the previous loop in place with a finger as you make the next stitch.

Pistil Stitch

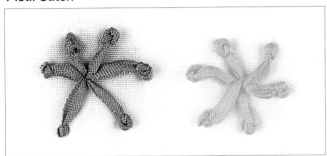

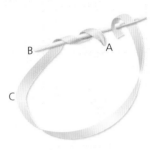

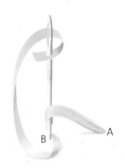

1 Several of these stitches can be worked in a circle to form a flower head. Bring the ribbon up at A. Wrap the ribbon twice, clockwise, around the needle. Insert the point of the needle at B, holding the ribbon at C to maintain tension.

2 Twist the needle into an upright position and pull the ribbon through to the back.

Back Stitch Rose

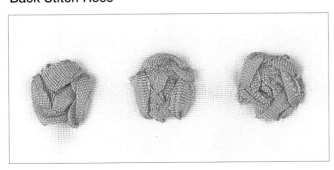

Start with two small straight stitches in the center. To make the petals, make a spiral of back stitches from A to B, C to D, etc, in a clockwise direction, increasing their length until the rose is the required size.

Gathered Rose

stitches along one edge of an 8 in (20 cm) length of ¼ in (7 mm) ribbon. Leave a long end on the gathering thread. Stitch the other end of the ribbon to the background fabric. Then pull up the gathering thread to form ¾ in (2 cm) of ruffles.

1 The size of this rose can be varied with different lengths and widths of ribbon. Using matching sewing thread, work a row of tiny running

2 Stab stitch the gathered edge of the ribbon onto the fabric in a tight coil to make the rose. Take the ribbon to the wrong side of the fabric to secure it.

Spider's Web Rose

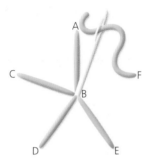

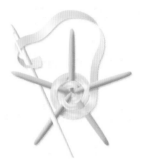

allowing it to twist slightly. When the rose is complete, take the ribbon to the wrong side to secure.

1 This rose is created by weaving a length of ribbon under and over a foundation of straight stitches. Using matching embroidery thread, work five evenly spaced straight stitch spokes into the same central point.

2 Bring the ribbon up close to the center and, working in a counterclockwise direction, take the needle alternately under and over the foundation stitches without piercing the fabric. Pull the ribbon around gently,

Merrilyn Bow

and bring the point out at B; loop the ribbon under the point of the needle and gently pull the needle through; make a small stitch to C. Make a second detached chain stitch from A to D.

1 This charming bow was devised by ribbon embroidery expert, Merrilyn Heazlewood. Bring the ribbon up at A. Work a large detached chain stitch – insert the needle at A

2 Make the tails of the bow with two long stitches from A to E and A to F, twisting the ribbon to give a more natural look. Finish the bow with a small slanting stitch across the center at A.

Key
◊ Ribbon stitch
◊ Side ribbon stitch
◊ Back-to-back ribbon
    stitch
§ Twisted chain stitch
◊ Loop stitch
◊ Pistel stitch
◎ Back stitch rose in
    orange ribbon
❀ Gathered rose in ¼ in
    (7 mm) light turquoise
    ribbon
◎ Spider's web rose in ¼ in
    (7 mm) lilac ribbon
◦ French knot
◊ Straight stitch in pale
    green (369) and dark
    green (699) coton à
    broder
❀ Merrilyn bow in ⅜ in
    (10 mm) orange ribbon

Silk Ribbon floral panel stitch diagram: actual size

How to Stitch the Silk Ribbon Floral Panel

Silk ribbon embroidery lends itself well to floral designs, and this naturalistic posy includes all the stitches featured in this section. The flowers, petals and leaves are worked in different widths of silk ribbon to give variety, and translucent organza ribbon was used for the bow.

You will need

8 x 10 in (20 x 25 cm) white cotton fabric

8 x 10 in (20 x 25 cm) stretcher frame

Thumbtacks or staple gun

DMC coton à broder, 1 skein each of pale green 369 and dark green 699

20 in (50 cm) x ¼ in (7 mm) silk ribbon in lilac, light turquoise and light green

20 in (50 cm) x ⅛ in (4 mm) silk ribbon in red, mid-green and blue

40 in (1 m) x ⅛ in (4 mm) silk ribbon in yellow and orange

20 in (50 cm) x ⅜ in (10 mm) orange organza ribbon

Sewing thread in lilac and light turquoise

Long-eyed needle

6¾ x 8 in (17 x 20 cm) cotton batting

6 x 7 in (15 x 18 cm) mat board

PVA adhesive

Preparing the fabric

1 Transfer the design on page 71 to a central position on the fabric (pages 7–8).

2 Tack the fabric onto the frame (page 6).

Stitching the design

1 First work the flower stalks in stem stitch and the ferny leaves in straight stitch, using two strands of the light and dark green coton à broder.

2 Make the spokes for the spider's web rose in the lilac sewing thread. Then weave the petals with ¼ in (7 mm) lilac ribbon.

3 Work the large flower in back-to-back ribbon stitch with ¼ in (7 mm) light turquoise ribbon.

4 Gather the remaining length of ¼ in (7 mm) light turquoise ribbon and make the gathered rose.

5 Stitch the straight stitch leaves in ¼ in (7 mm) light green ribbon.

6 Stitch the remaining flowers and leaves in ⅛ in (4 mm) ribbon, following the stitch diagram and add a few French knots in ⅛ in (4 mm) ribbon on the right-hand side.

7 Finish off with a Merrilyn bow in the orange organza ribbon.

Mounting the panel

1 Remove the embroidery from the frame.

2 Glue the batting to the mat board and trim the corners.

3 Place the embroidery centrally over the batting. Turn the surplus fabric to the back of the board and lace it securely (page 8).

4 Mount in a deep picture frame.

Stumpwork

Stumpwork, or raised work, reached a creative peak in England at the end of the seventeenth century. It combines a wide range of embroidery and needlelace stitches, often wired and padded, to create three-dimensional images and was used on specially constructed caskets, mirrors and framed panels. The scenes and vignettes depicted in the 1680s were naturalistic and quirky, often featuring biblical or historical characters set amid improbable flora and fauna with a charming disregard for true scale and proportion. More than three centuries later, stumpwork is undergoing an enthusiastic revival. Around the mid-1980s, textile artists began to re-interpret the techniques using traditional and modern materials. The apparent intricacy of stumpwork can be intimidating, but it is built up gradually with a variety of separate elements and different stitches. Start with some of the basic stitches to develop your skills and then enjoy the inventiveness of stumpwork.

FABRICS
A mid- to heavyweight muslin makes a good neutral background; the cotton fabric will support the applied elements and will not clash with the threads. If silk or satin fabric is preferred, mount it on a piece of muslin for extra strength (page 6). Extra color and depth can be added with fabric paints or crayons.

THREADS
Depending on the size of stitch and the effect required, almost any thread can be used for stumpwork, including stranded embroidery floss, coton à broder, flower thread and pearl cotton. Twisted threads give more definition to the stitches so use fine crochet thread or *fil à dentelles* for needlelace. You could also experiment with some of the more unusual glittery or space-dyed threads.

NEEDLES
A selection will be needed for various purposes: large-eyed embroidery or crewel needles for most stitching; ballpoint or small tapestry needles for needlelace; and fine sharp needles for sewing on beads or spangles.

OTHER TOOLS AND MATERIALS
Stumpwork should always be mounted in a frame and a free-standing one that leaves both hands free makes stitching easier and quicker. Brass or colored beading wire and tissue-covered wire from a cake decorating supplier are used to stiffen the edges of needlelace motifs. You will need a pair of wire-cutters for these. Couronnes (see below) can be worked over any dowel or cylindrical object, but specially-turned graduated wooden ring sticks make the task easier. Padded shapes can be worked over craft felt or heavy interfacing, both bonded materials that do not fray. Select felt in a color to match the thread or apply fabric paint to interfacing for the same results.

USES
Stumpwork has always been worked for display, rather than practicality.

Getting Started

It is always helpful for the beginner to make a sampler to practice new techniques, and with stumpwork it is important to become familiar with working the raised and padded stitches. Try out the stitches and techniques below in different threads and on different scales to see just how much potential for creativity there is. To protect your work, pin a piece of cotton fabric or a clean handkerchief over each section of the embroidery as it is completed. It is so easy to snag a raised thread and difficult to put it right without re-working it. Needlewoven petals and raised leaves are especially vulnerable.

How to make stumpwork stitches

Plain and Spiral Cordonettes

A cordonette consists of buttonhole stitch worked over a thread or wire foundation. Come up at A and loop the thread from left to right. Slide the needle behind the ring from B to C, pull it through the loop and draw up the thread. Repeat to the end, easing the

bottom of each stitch flat. To finish off, pass the needle through the base of the first stitch and then through the back of a few stitches. For a spiral cordonette, allow each stitch to sit above the previous one to form a spiraling ridge.

Couronne (also known as Crown or Flying Flowers)

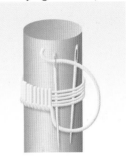
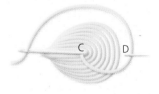

These smaller buttonholed rings are traditionally made over a graduated stick, but a pencil or knitting needle is equally effective. Holding a spare needle against the stick, wind the foundation thread around it several times. Work buttonhole stitch (page 41) over the

threads and the loose end. Remove the spare needle as the couronne becomes tighter. Slip it off the stick and finish off as for a cordonette.

Raised Leaf

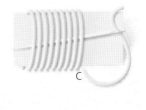

1 This is formed from a series of flattened loops, anchored with a detached chain stitch. Cut a narrow strip of thin card and hold it on edge along the center line of the leaf. Starting from A to B, work several closely spaced stitches taking the thread over the card and through the fabric.

2 Come up at C and slide the needle under the stitches. Remove the card and gently press the loops down to the right.

3 Take the needle back down at C and bring the point up at D, over the working thread. Pull the thread through and finish with a short straight stitch.

Needlewoven Picot

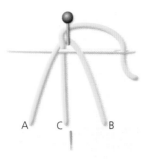

loop. Bring the needle up at C and take the working thread behind the pin head. Weave the needle under the right loop, over the center thread and under the left loop from right to left.
2 Weave the needle back from left to right, going over the loop and under the center. Continue weaving downwards until the loop is filled, keeping the tension

1 Using a firm thread, start by making a loop the size of the finished picot, from A to B. Insert a pin to secure the

even. Take the thread down at C and fasten off. Remove the pin.

Banksia Rose (also known as Raised Rose)

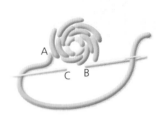

1 Choose a shade of yellow thread for the heart of this naturalistic stitch and make four small looped stitches over a fine knitting needle.

2 With a second color, come up close to the center. Work a loose stem stitch from A to B, the same height as the yellow loops. Come up again

at C to start the next stitch and continue stitching in a spiral, pulling each successive round a little tighter to form a dome shape.

Burden Stitch

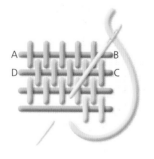

This versatile filling can be shaded by varying the color of the upright stitches. Lay the horizontal foundation threads across the shape to be filled from A to B, C to D,

etc. Starting at the top left corner, work rows of interlocking vertical stitches over each thread in turn.

Raised Stem Band

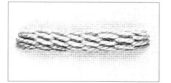

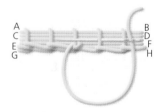

Use this composite stitch for solid straight lines. It works best with twisted thread. Lay several closely-spaced satin stitches along the line to be worked, from A to B and C to D, etc. Couch these down at regular intervals with

straight stitches worked at right angles. Finish off by working stem stitch (page 29) over the couching stitches, from H to G, then back from E, until the foundation threads are concealed.

Velvet Stitch

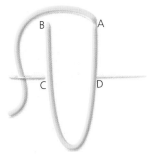

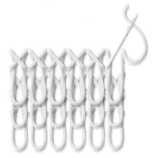

1 Primarily a canvas stitch, this will add texture to stumpwork designs. Use stranded embroidery floss to create a fluffy pile. Starting at the bottom left corner of the area, make a loop from A to B. Come back up at A, down at C and up again at D.

2 Complete the tight cross stitch by taking the needle down at B. Come back up at E to start the next stitch on the row.

3 Continue working upwards in rows to fill the space. Then cut and trim the loops.

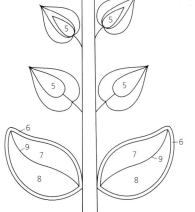

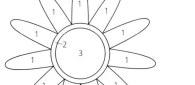

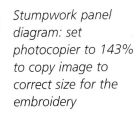

Stumpwork panel diagram: set photocopier to 143% to copy image to correct size for the embroidery

Key

1 Needlewoven picot in yellow (742) coton à broder
2 Couronne in orange (51) coton perlé
3 Velvet stitch in brown (632) coton à broder
4 Raised stem band in olive (94) coton perlé
5 Raised leaf stitch in olive (94) coton perlé
6 Spiral cordonette in olive (94) fil à dentelles
7 Double Brussels stitch in olive (94) coton perlé
8 Cloth stitch in olive (94) coton perlé
9 Plain cordonette in olive (94) fil à dentelles
10 Stem stitch in pale coral (3778) coton perlé
11 Banksia rose in yellow (743) coton perlé (centre) and deep pink (3687) or pale pink (3688) coton perlé (petals)
12 Needlewoven picot in olive (94) fil à dentelles
13 Padded cloth stitch in pale coral (3778) coton perlé
14 Burden stitch in pale coral (3778) and deep coral (3830) coton perlé

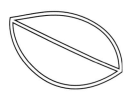

Leaf template: actual size

How to Stitch the Stumpwork Panel

This cheerful sunflower in a rose-filled terracotta pot makes an ideal introduction to stumpwork. It incorporates all the stitches you have learned and the free-standing lower leaves, which have wired edges, are made from needlelace. The design has a fresh, contemporary feel, which is well displayed under an oval mat.

You will need

12 x 16 in (30 x 40 cm) cream muslin
Embroidery frame or large hoop
DMC coton perlé No. 8, 1 skein of each
    of the following colors:
Orange (51)
Olive (94)
Yellow (743)
Deep pink (3687)
Pale pink (3688)
Pale coral (3778)
Deep coral (3830)
DMC coton à broder No. 16, 1 skein of
    each of the following colors:
Yellow (742)
Brown (632)
DMC *fil à dentelles* No. 80, 1 skein of
    green (94)
Bead container or other round object,
    1 in (2.5 cm) in diameter
Selection of needles
Tissue-covered wire
Coral craft paint
¾ in (2 cm) strip of thin card
Scrap of heavy Pellon
Piece of cardboard or hardboard to fit
    the frame
Oval mat (optional)
Frame

> *Needlelace stitches are often used in stumpwork as well as many free embroidery stitches, e.g. French and bullion knots, padded satin, stem, and long and short stitch, seeding and spider's webs. Rocaille, bugle and seed beads and tiny sequins can be used with discretion as shiny highlights.*

Preparing the fabric

1 Enlarge and transfer the design outline on page 77 onto the center of the fabric using tissue paper (page 8). For the leaves, mark only the positions of the central veins.
2 Mount the fabric in a frame or hoop.

Stitching the design

1 Refer to the stitch diagram and key throughout when working the design. Start with the sunflower head. To make the couronne foundation, wind the thread around the 1 in (2.5 cm) diameter bead container. Wind plenty of thread so that the couronne will be well padded and then work the buttonhole stitch. Stab stitch it in place at several points around the edge.
2 Fill the center of the couronne with velvet stitch, working in concentric circles rather than rows, starting around the outside and working inwards.
3 Start the base of the needlewoven picot petals against the couronne and place the pin at the outer tip. Complete each petal in turn.
4 Using the leaf template (page 77) as a guide and reversing the right-hand leaf, make the two needlelace leaves over cordonettes of fine wire. Work the upper parts in single Brussels stitch (page 135) and the lower parts in cloth stitch (page 136). Make a straight plain cordonette along the center of each leaf and then work a spiral cordonette around the edges. Stitch the two leaves in position on the stem line and shape the wire gently. Pin fabric over the flower and leaves to protect them.
5 Sew the raised stem band stalk, working the top end under the petals.
6 Work the raised leaves over a ¾ in (2 cm) strip of card, winding the thread 13 times for the smaller and 16 times for the larger leaves.
7 Work the line along the back of the flowerpot in stem stitch (page 29) and the lower part of the pot in two shades of burden stitch to give a three-dimensional look. Cut a piece of heavy Pellon for the rim of the pot and paint it to match the pale coral thread. Baste it in place and work cloth stitch over this padding.
8 Fill the pot with Banksia roses and needlewoven picot leaves.

Mounting the embroidery

1 Remove the embroidery from the frame and trim the fabric so it is 2 in (5 cm) larger all around than the hardboard to go in the frame.
2 Lace the fabric over the hardboard (page 8) and place the finished panel in the frame covered by an oval mat if wished.

Shadow Work

Like much other stitchery, contemporary shadow work evolved from a traditional white-on-white technique. Also known as Etruscan work, its origins can be traced back to the needlelaces that were made in imitation of costly bobbin laces, but which developed into an independent form of embroidery. It was worked in linen thread on the finest voile, in both Europe and America. The designs were outlined in closed herringbone stitch and filled with intricate drawn thread patterns.

In modern shadow work, herringbone stitch is used by itself and in combination with back stitch, particularly in India where it has been produced on a commercial scale. It is stitched from the right side of the fabric so that parts of the design appear to be outlined in back stitch. The long, crossed threads of the herringbone stitch lie on the wrong side and show through the sheer background fabric as blocks of muted color. The effect is delicate and ethereal, and the technique offers great scope for imaginative exploration using different threads and fabrics.

FABRICS

The fabric has to be fine and transparent so that the stitches on the reverse are clearly visible, while being substantial enough to support the embroidery without sagging or splitting. Look for strong, sheer fabrics with a close, firm weave in natural or synthetic fibers: voile, organza and silk chiffon all work well.

THREADS

Dark colors are most visually dramatic and show through the fabric well, but lighter shades can be used to create a more pastel effect. The thicker the thread, the stronger the "filling" of the motif will appear, but very heavy stitches will look clumsy. The finest coton à broder, silk and pearl cotton threads are easy to use and give a bold back-stitched outline. Stranded embroidery floss is very versatile: use anything from two to six strands to vary the density of the embroidery.

NEEDLES

Long-eyed embroidery needles will accommodate most threads: choose one that is the right size to take the thread through the fabric without parting the weave and creating a series of holes.

USES

Shadow work has long been used to embellish domestic items such as dainty napkins, baby clothes and lawn handkerchiefs, but on a larger scale it is ideal for use on curtains or window screens where its translucent qualities can be appreciated.

Preparing the fabric

Cut a piece of your chosen fabric, allowing at least 2 in (5 cm) extra all around. Finish the edges of the fabric to prevent them from fraying (page 6).

Shadow embroidery should always be worked in an embroidery hoop or frame, so that an even tension is maintained and the long herringbone stitches do not become tight and pucker the fabric. An embroidery hoop is ideal for working small designs or isolated motifs scattered over a large area. Mount the fabric carefully, keeping the warp and weft straight (page 6), but do not pull it too hard or tighten the frame too much, or the weave may become distorted or damaged.

Getting started

It is worth taking time to try out a sample piece before embarking on any embroidery project, and this is especially true with shadow work, where the comparative weights of the fabric and thread must be perfectly matched for a good finish. Stitch with a regular tension, keeping the back stitches even, and avoid pulling the thread too tightly.

Starting and finishing

The ends of the thread must be secured as unobtrusively as possible on a sheer background fabric. Start with a couple of small running stitches along the design line. Anchor the thread with a double back stitch, piercing the first stitch with the needle when working the second. Finish the end of a line by making two small half hitches over the end of the last herringbone stitch, close to the outline. Clip all the threads short, keeping any excess within the shape of the motif.

Working curves

The closed herringbone stitch instructions show how to work the basic stitch between two parallel lines, but most designs have flowing curves and rounded forms. To work within these outlines and to accommodate the curves, the length of the back stitches has to be varied. There will always be the same number of back stitches at the top and bottom of a motif, so on an inside curve the stitches have to be shorter and on an outside curve they are longer.

Working a curved shape

Working points

Always start at the most pointed end of a shape. Make the first two stitches meet to form a point. Keep the two rows of back stitch close together and gradually let them diverge to follow the widening outline, before bringing them back together at the other end of the shape. If the motif has a rounded end, work herringbone stitch as far as possible and then finish with one or two back stitches to complete the design line.

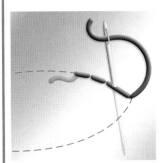

Starting

Finishing

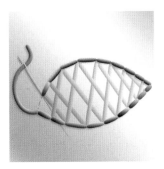

Completing the design line

How to make the shadow work stitch

Closed Herringbone Stitch

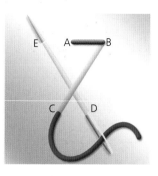

Work from right to left, starting with a back stitch from A to B. Bring the needle up diagonally down at C, half a stitch length from directly below A. Insert it at D, directly below the center of the first stitch. Bring it out, a stitch length from A, at E. Take it back down at A to make the next back stitch on the top line. Continue making pairs of back stitches, alternately on the top and bottom lines. The shorter the herringbone stitches, the denser the color will be.

Lavender bag motif and stitch diagram: actual size

How to Stitch the Lavender Bag

Crystal organza makes a perfect background fabric for this simple French lavender motif, and its subtle sparkle offsets the strong colors of the stranded embroidery floss. Fill the bag with dried lavender, potpourri or rose petals to enjoy the fragrance in your closet or linen cupboard.

You will need

12 in (30 cm) square white crystal organza

8 in (20 cm) embroidery hoop

DMC stranded embroidery floss, 1 skein of each of the following colors:

Blue (519)

Purple (550)

Lilac (553)

Green (906)

Turquoise (3809)

Embroidery needle

12 x 18 in (30 x 45 cm) fine white cotton fabric

18 in (45 cm) x ⅜ in (1cm) wide white grosgrain ribbon

Matching sewing thread

Key

1 Lilac 553

2 Purple 550

3 Green 906

4 Turquoise 3809

5 Blue 519

Working the design

1 Transfer the motif opposite, placing it centrally on the organza (page 7).

2 Bind the edges of the fabric and mount it in a bound embroidery hoop (page 6).

3 Work the embroidery in three strands of embroidery floss, following the stitch diagram and key opposite. Use closed herringbone stitch for the flower heads, leaves and bow and back stitch for the stems.

Making the lavender pocket

1 Remove the finished embroidery from the hoop. Iron it lightly on the wrong side, using a pressing cloth to protect the fabric.

2 With right sides together, pin and baste one short end of the cotton fabric to the top edge of the organza. Machine stitch ⅜ in (1 cm) from the edge and then press the seam allowance towards the cotton.

3 Fold the cotton to the back of the organza and baste the two layers together along the bottom and then the side edges. Mark the center of the bottom edge with a pin. Then press a fold along the top edge to form a cuff.

4 Join the two side edges with a narrow French seam. With the bag still wrong sides out, match the base of the seam to the marker pin. Pin, baste and machine stitch the bottom edge to make a bag.

5 Turn the bag right sides out and fill it with scented petals or lavender. Then tie the ribbon just below the cotton cuff.

Insertion Stitching

Insertion stitching is as much a dressmaking technique as a form of embroidery. Also known as faggoting, it is a useful way to join two edges of fabric, using decorative stitches rather than a seam. It was originally born out of necessity: at a time when hand looms could only produce narrow widths of fabric, the strips had to be sewn together before they could be made into garments, bed sheets and other household items. Over centuries several open, lacy stitches have developed from the original, simple veining. Insertion stitching has often been used in conjunction with drawn thread embroidery and other open work on linen, whitework and children's clothing. More glamorously, hand-made satin lingerie and silk housecoats of the 1930s were often trimmed with narrow bias piping or braid attached with insertion stitching.

FABRICS
Any two fabrics, from evenweave linen to the finest cotton lawn, can be joined with faggoting, provided a thread of suitable weight is used.

THREADS
Twisted threads such as coton à broder or crochet thread will produce a firm stitch and give the best finish, whereas stranded embroidery floss and silks are too soft. Choose a thread that is slightly thicker than the fabric so that the stitches will stand out well.

NEEDLES
Use a sharp-pointed crewel or embroidery needle, which should suit most threads and fabrics, in a size to suit the weight of the fabric.

USES
Insertion stitching is an attractive option for many projects and can be worked in place of straight, diagonal or curved seams. Use it to add a border to a tray cloth, incorporate an embroidered panel into a baby's garment or attach a false hem to a little girl's skirt. It can also be used to sew squares of fabric together as an embellished variation on basic patchwork.

Preparing the fabric

Finish each of the two edges to be joined with a folded hem, either neatly machine-stitched, slipstitched by hand or, for a really ornate look, worked with an open hem stitch. Alternatively, two selvages can be joined.

The main concern when working insertion stitches is to keep the space between the two pieces of fabric consistent. To do this, mount them temporarily on a firm background before

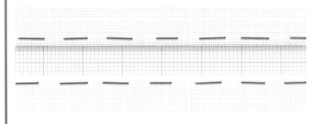

Using graph paper to maintain an even tension

they are sewn together. Simply baste the two edges onto a sheet of paper, leaving the required space between them – the heavier the fabric and thicker the thread, the wider the gap required.

You may find that you need to give the fabrics a little more support in order to maintain an even tension for your first pieces. Glue a sheet of graph paper onto thin cardboard to use as the backing. As well as helping to space the fabrics, the grid will provide a useful guide for keeping the individual stitches the same length and evenly spaced.

Starting and finishing

Start and finish each thread securely. Traditionally, a small bar of buttonhole stitch (page 41) was worked at the beginning and end of each row to keep the edges firm. When the work is complete, cut the basting threads and remove the fabric from the backing.

How to make insertion stitches

Cretan Insertion Stitch (also known as Faggoting)

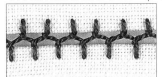
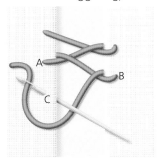

This is the simplest of all insertion stitches. Take the needle down at A, come up in the gap and make a stitch diagonally down to the right, taking the needle down at B. Come up in the gap, over the previous stitch. Make a stitch, taking the needle

down at C, below A. Come up again over the previous stitch as before. Continue making pairs of sloping stitches to the end.

Twisted Insertion Stitch (also known as Twisted Faggoting)

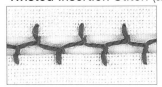
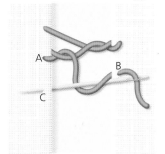

A variation of Cretan insertion, this stitch has one extra twist at the beginning of each stitch and the needle always comes through from the back. Bring the needle up at A and make a stitch diagonally downwards to bring the needle up at B.

Twist the needle under and over the previous stitch and come up at C. Twist the needle around the previous stitch as before and continue to the end.

Knotted Insertion Stitch (also known as Knotted Faggoting)

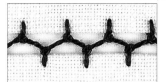

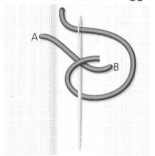

under the needle point. Gently pull the thread through to form a knot.

2 Take the needle down at C and come up over the

1 Come up at A and make a stitch down to the right, taking the needle down at B. Come up in the gap, over the previous stitch, and loop the thread from left to right

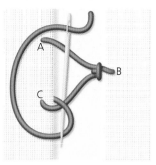

previous stitch as before. This time loop the thread from right to left under the needle point and then form the second knot. Continue alternating the stitches to the end of the row.

Faggot Bundles (also known as Insertion Bundles)

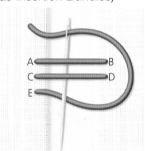

and pass it behind the two previous stitches and over the working thread.

1 This knotted stitch must be worked with consistent tension to produce a regular effect. Make two horizontal stitches from A to B and C to D. Bring the needle up at E

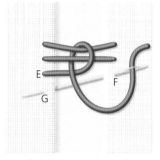

2 Pull the thread through, drawing the stitches together and take the needle down at F. Start the next bundle at G.

Buttonhole Insertion Stitch

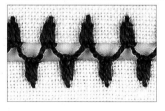

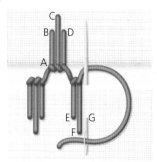

Sets of three buttonhole stitches are worked alternately from one piece of fabric to the other. Starting at A, take the needle down B and bring the point out at the edge at A. Wrap the working thread around the needle point and pull the needle through to complete the first buttonhole stitch. Work the second stitch, from C, slightly longer and the third, from D, the same length as the first.

Now start the second set of buttonhole stitches on the other piece of fabric, at E, turning the work if necessary. Remember to make the longer stitch from F and complete with the third stitch from G. Continue working alternating sets of stitches to the end.

Laced Insertion Stitch (also known as Whipped Buttonhole Insertion Stitch)

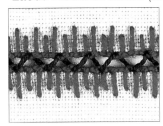

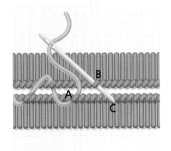

This stitch must be worked across a narrow gap between the two fabrics to keep the seam stable. Work a row of buttonhole stitch (page 41) along each of the edges to be joined. With the same or a contrasting color, take the needle down at A and bring it up in the gap. Make a short diagonal stitch, taking the needle down at B. Come up in the gap and make a diagonal stitch as before, taking the needle down at C. Repeat to the end, keeping the lacing even.

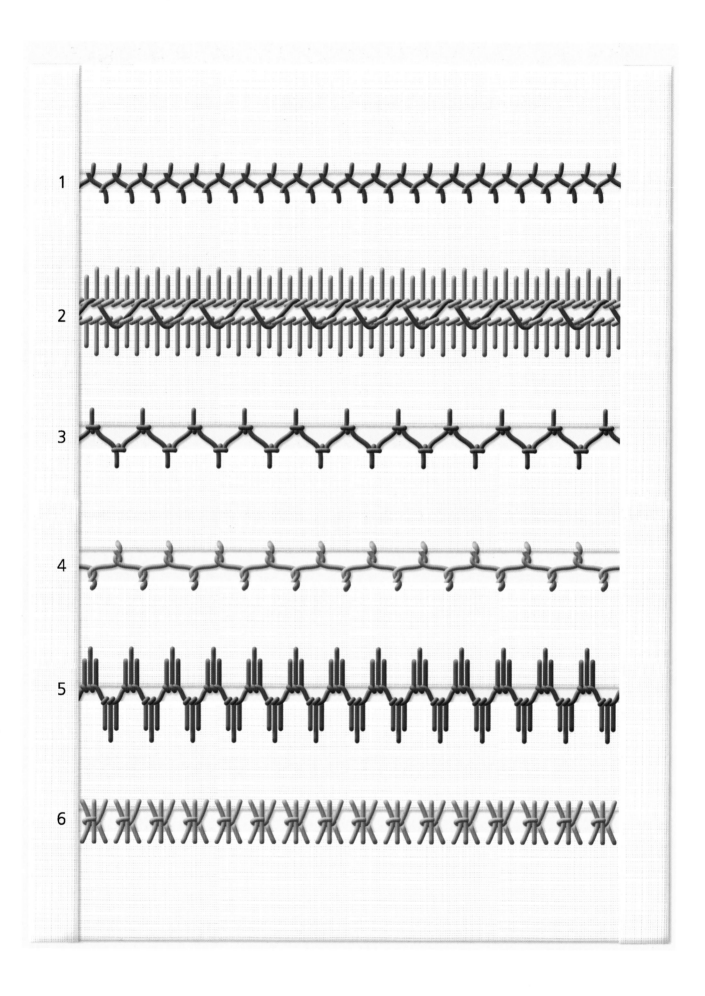

How to Stitch the Insertion Stitching Sampler

This small sampler of insertion stitching is worked in red and blue threads, which echo the colors used for the utilitarian darning samplers of the nineteenth century. To continue the practical theme, a new dishtowel proved a good source for the cream linen fabric.

You will need
Paper glue
Sheet of graph paper
6 x 8 in (15 x 20 cm) thin cardboard
6 x 12 in (15 x 30 cm) heavy linen
Basting thread
DMC coton perlé No. 5, 1 skein of
    each of the following colors:
Red (321)
Dark blue (796)
3¼ x 8 in (8 x 20 cm) ticking, stripes
    running widthwise
Sewing needle
Crewel needle

Key
Band 1 Twisted insertion stitch in dark blue 796
Band 2 Laced insertion stitch in red 321 and dark blue 796
Band 3 Knotted insertion stitch in dark blue 796
Band 4 Cretan insertion stitch in red 321
Band 5 Buttonhole insertion stitch in dark blue 796
Band 6 Faggot bundles in red 321

Preparing the materials
1 Glue the graph paper onto the cardboard to make the backing.
2 Cut seven 1⅝ x 5¼ in (4 x 13 cm) strips from the linen. Press under a ⅜ in (1 cm) allowance along each long edge. Beginning ¾ in (2 cm) from the top edge, baste the strips onto the backing, aligning them directly below each other and leaving ³⁄₁₆ in (5 mm) gaps between them.

Stitching the sampler
1 Following the diagram and key, work the six rows of insertion stitching. Start and finish each row ³⁄₁₆ in (5 mm) from the edges.
2 When the stitching is complete, carefully unpick the basting stitches and trim the raw side edges as necessary to square them up.

Trimming the sampler
1 To make the side borders, cut two 1½ x 8 in (3.5 x 19 cm) strips of ticking. Baste under a ³⁄₁₆ in (5 mm) allowance along one long edge of each strip. With right sides and raw edges together, baste one strip to each side of the finished sampler.
2 Turn under the short ends of the ticking and then fold the strips over to enclose the raw edges of the sampler. Baste each strip down and then slipstitch it into place.

Insertion stitching sampler stitch diagram

Net Embroidery

Net embroidery, with patterns stitched directly into the delicate mesh of a piece of netting, was originally a substitute for handmade bobbin lace. As textile manufacture became mechanized and looms that could weave wide netting were invented, a thriving craft developed. Patterns and instructions appeared in needlework books and magazines from the 1880s onwards, and embroidered net was used to decorate dresses or baby clothes and to edge bonnets and shawls. The floral and geometric designs, all embroidered in white on white, were usually based on the hexagonal mesh pattern of the net ground. Contemporary net embroidery pushes the boundaries farther, using subtle or bold colors to re-interpret the traditional stitches.

FABRIC

Silk net, specially made for veiling, has the most regular mesh, but it can prove expensive. Nylon net, which comes in fine and medium-sized mesh and many bright colors as well as white, is cheaper and much more readily available. All net tears quite easily so it needs careful handling.

THREADS

Use sewing thread, stranded rayon or cotton embroidery threads, silk twist or fine coton à broder, depending on the weight of the net. A combination of threads can look very effective, with a heavy thread used for outlining and a finer one for details.

NEEDLES

Use a blunt-ended needle, either ballpoint or fine tapestry, that is fine enough to pass easily through the mesh when threaded.

USES

Apart from the obvious choice of embellishing a bridal veil, net embroidery can also be used to decorate a special outfit for a new baby or an evening dress. Small motifs make effective greeting cards, and larger panels can be mounted in box frames or simply framed without backing to be set against a window.

Preparing the fabric

The hexagonal mesh of nylon netting is not perfectly symmetrical and may not be lined up with the side edges, so you must make allowance for this. Cut the fabric carefully, first following one line of holes to get a straight edge. Then cut at right angles to this edge.

Narrow lengths of net can be held in the hand, but larger pieces are easier to stitch if they are in a frame. The net is so delicate that it cannot be put under much tension, so pin or staple it onto a wooden stretcher frame, like those used for artists' canvas, for the best results. Line up one straight edge of the net along the side of the frame to keep it regular.

Getting started

Always work with a long length of thread, at least 30 in (75 cm) long, to avoid having to make too many seams in the work. Start by leaving a long end which can be darned in later and join in a new length by darning in and out of the last ¾ in (15 mm) of the previous line. Clip secured ends close to the work.

Running, satin, eyelet and herringbone stitches can all be worked on net. Because the thread on both the right and the wrong side is visible, the stitches look quite different from those worked on fabric. Buttonhole stitch can also be used to make a scalloped edging (page 105) when a narrow lacy finish is required. Work all stitches fairly loosely, with an even tension, so that they do not distort the net.

Symmetrical motifs can be worked as counted thread designs by following and counting the number of holes worked in each direction. More flowing designs can be drawn onto heavy tracing or architect's paper and basted behind the net.

How to make net embroidery stitches

Running Stitch

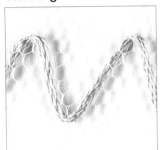
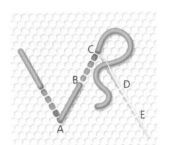

This can be stitched geometrically, following the rows of holes in the net, or more freely over the lines of a traced pattern. The individual stitches can be tiny, worked in and out of adjacent holes, or longer as shown here. To work the zigzag, bring the needle up at A and, following the hexagonal grid of the net, insert the needle at B. Come up at C and make the next stitch to D. Come back up at E to continue.

Net Darning

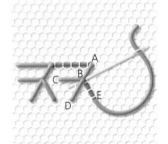

Intricate branched patterns can be formed by darning backwards and forwards from the same foundation line. To work this pattern, make a straight stitch from A to B. Come up again at C and make a stitch back to B.

Make two more similar stitches from D and E. Come up at A to continue the foundation line and the branching pattern to the end of the row.

Herringbone Stitch

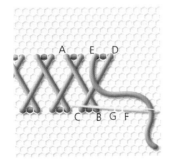

This is worked in the same way as for surface embroidery, but because the thread on both sides of the net can be seen, it looks like a continuous looped stitch. Bring the needle up at A and make a long stitch that slopes along the grid down to B. Come up again at C, two threads of net to the left of B, and then make a long stitch to D, four net threads to the right of A. Come up again at E, two net threads to the left of D. Repeat this pattern to complete the row.

Key

1 Net darning in blanc
2 Net darning in pale lilac 342
3 Running stitch in pale lilac 342
4 Net darning in mid-blue 3755
5 Net darning in turquoise 30813
6 Net darning in pale purple 30554
7 Herringbone stitch in pale blue 3752
8 Net darning in pale lilac 210

How to Stitch the Snowflake Panel

Worked in frosty shades of blue, white and lilac, this net panel could be mounted within a box frame or onto a simple square frame to prop against a window. The hexagonal motifs are darned onto the net and some have extra running stitch detail. Try practicing the stitches on a bit of net before working the project – a single snowflake could decorate a Christmas card or gift tag.

You will need
16 in (40 cm) square of net
10 in (25 cm) square stretcher frame
Thumbtacks or staple gun
DMC stranded embroidery floss,
    1 skein in each of the following
    colors:
Blanc
Lilac (210)
Pale lilac (342)
Mid-blue (3755)
Pale blue (3752)
DMC rayon floss, 1 skein in each
    of the following colors:
Turquoise (30813)
Pale purple (30554)
Small tapestry needle

Preparing the net
1 Cut a 10 in (25 cm) square of net with the direction of the mesh running parallel to one edge. Then pin or staple the net to the frame.
2 Enlarge the stitch diagram below on a photocopier. Trim it to fit within the frame and baste it to the back of the net. Alternatively, the motifs can be worked freehand, by counting the holes in the net mesh.

Working the design
1 First work the top and bottom borders in herringbone stitch.
2 Work the snowflakes in net darning and running stitch as indicated on the stitch diagram and key.
3 Carefully remove the net from the frame and mount it as desired.

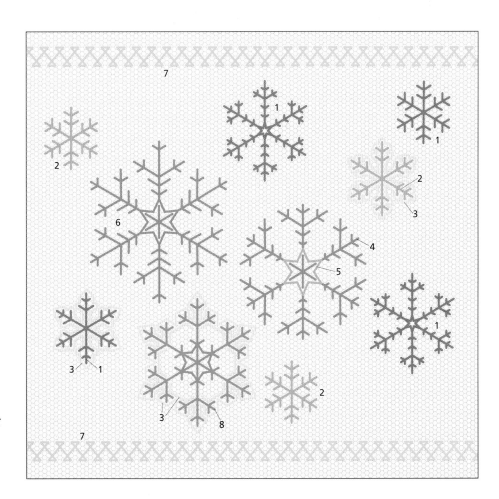

Snowflake panel stitch diagram: set photocopier to 165% to copy image to correct size for the embroidery

Metallic Thread Work

Sumptuous and opulent, embroidery worked in gold, silver and other metallic threads has been associated with ceremonial display, ecclesiastical dress and extravagance for many centuries. The costliness of the threads lead to a degree of mystique surrounding the techniques, which were once only practiced in professional workshops. Now, threads are made from polyester or coiled, plated copper wires, rather than beaten pure gold, and they are fascinating and easy to work with.

FABRICS

Metallic thread embroidery is usually done on a ground of lustrous silk or satin, with a cotton backing to support the weight of the heavy threads. Interesting results can also be achieved with upholstery fabrics and dressmaking materials such as metallic organza or velvet.

THREADS

Most metallic threads are too thick to pass through the background fabric and are stitched down onto the surface (called "couching"). There are two main types: hollow purl threads and solid couched threads. For the couching, use silk or cotton sewing thread, in a shade that either matches or contrasts with the metallic thread, depending on the effect required. Run the thread over beeswax to strengthen it. Metallic pearl thread is available and metallic floss can be couched down or separated out and stitched through the fabric. Machine embroidery threads are good for fine details.

Purl threads are made of different types of fine wire coiled around a form. Longer pieces are couched and short lengths are stitched like beads. Each type comes in several thicknesses: smooth purl or bullion brilliant is like narrow shiny spring; rough purl or bullion matt has a duller finish; pearl purl or jaceron resembles a string of tiny pearls; and check purl or frieze brilliant is sparkly and faceted.

Couched threads are made of a fine wire or narrow foil spun around a central core. As they tend to unravel, wind a short length of cellophane tape around the point to be cut. Smooth passing (wire bound around a cotton core) is used singly, while two lengths of Japan thread are usually couched together. Rococo and crinkle cordonnet are both wavy in appearance and grecian and twist (torsade) are thicker cords. Soutache and other narrow braids are used for heavier effects.

NEEDLES

A sharp, thick chenille needle with a long eye is used for piercing the background fabric when plunging couched threads; a between or embroidery needle for couching stitches; and a fine crewel needle for sewing cut purls.

OTHER TOOLS

Snipping metal inevitably blunts any blade, so keep a old pair of embroidery scissors just for this purpose. Alternatively use a short craft knife. Cut purl threads on a piece of thick cardboard covered with a piece of velvet, to prevent the threads from shooting off in all directions. A pointed stiletto is useful for plunging the ends of couched threads. Use tweezers, rather than fingers, to pick up threads so that they do not tarnish so readily. There is also a tool called a mellore for easing threads into position and piercing holes.

USES

As a symbol of rank, gold embroidery has adorned everything from church vestments and court dress to heraldic banners and military epaulets. On a more domestic scale it can be used to decorate evening bags, throws and shawls, and for panels. Only small areas of metallic thread work are needed to create an impressive decoration.

Getting started

Metallic thread must be stitched onto firm fabric that is under even tension in a rectangular slate frame (rather than a hoop) to prevent the work from puckering. If a delicate background is to be used, first mount a piece of preshrunk muslin in the frame and then stitch the lighter fabric centrally onto this support (page 6).

Plunging couched threads

To maximize the amount of thread that can be used, the ends of couched threads are cut quite short. They are taken through to the wrong side of the work and neatly secured there. For finer threads, take a thick chenille needle halfway down into the fabric, close to the end of the stitching and thread the loose end of couched thread through the eye. Pull the thread to the wrong side and, using sewing thread, overcast the end to the adjacent stitches or fabric. Plunge each thread separately.

To plunge a cord, first tease the threads apart for a short distance at the raw end. Pierce holes with a stiletto at the end of the line and thread a needle with a double length of sewing thread. Bring the needle up through the hole, loop it over the ends of the cord and draw the loop down. Ease the ends through to the wrong side and secure them as above.

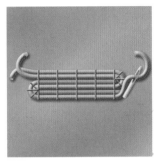

Plunging fine thread   Plunging cord

How to make metallic thread stitches

Double Thread Couching

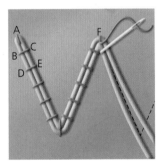

Cut a length of metallic thread a little longer than twice the length of the line

to be worked and fold it in half. Bring the couching thread up at A and make a straight stitch over the fold. Holding the two metallic threads together along the design line, work regularly spaced straight stitches in couching thread over them, making sure they lie flat. When the metallic threads turn a corner, such as at F,

couch each of them down separately. To finish, plunge the ends to the wrong side. Couch just one thread for a fine line. To make a thick line, use several threads together and plunge the ends with a loop.

Solid Couching

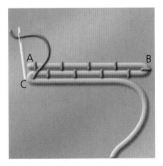

For a rectangular block, lay the metallic thread down from A to B and stitch it down in couching thread with vertical stitches. At the end of the line, turn the metallic thread and work one or more horizontal stitches, depending on the number of

metallic threads, across the thread at B. Continue to couch down continuous rows of metallic thread in the same way until the shape is complete. Finally, plunge the ends at the beginning and the end.

Spiral Couching

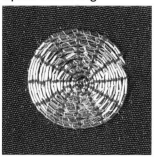

For a circle, mark intersection guidelines across the diameter. Starting at A, couch the metallic thread down around the perimeter, working the stitches along the guidelines and from the center outwards. Continue coiling the metallic thread to the center, keeping the couching stitches evenly spaced. Finally, plunge both ends.

Open Chain Couching

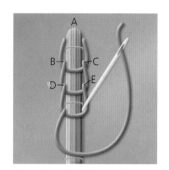

This flexible stitch is useful for wide outlines. Lay the metallic threads along the design line from A and couch them down with matching thread.

Then using an embroidery thread to match or contrast, work a line of open chain stitch over the metallic threads. Bring the needle up at B and take it down on the same level, at C making a loop. Bring the point up at D and take it down at E, through the previous loop. Repeat the sequence to complete the line and anchor the last loop with a short stitch at each corner.

Blanket Stitch Couching

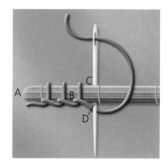

Another wide couching stitch, use this one for straight and curved lines. First, couch down the metallic threads as for open chain couching. Then work regularly spaced blanket stitch over them in a contrasting thread. Bring the needle up at B. Take it down again at C and come up directly below, at D, over the working thread. Repeat to finish the line, anchoring the final loop with a small straight stitch.

Attaching Purls

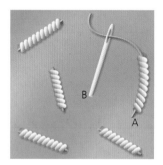

Lengths of any hollow thread can be sewn down in this way. Cut small lengths between ³⁄₁₆–⁵⁄₈ in (5–15 mm) and thread a fine needle with matching couching thread. Bring the needle up at A, slip on a purl and take the needle down at B, making sure the purl lies flat on the surface. Repeat over the area to be covered, varying the angles of the purls.

Padded Purl (also known as Guimped Work)

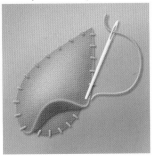

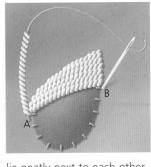

1 This technique is used for relief motifs. Cut two pieces of felt, one ¼ in (6 mm) smaller all around than the finished shape and the other 1/16 in (2 mm) smaller. Larger or more raised shapes may need more layers. Stab stitch down the small piece of felt in the center of the shape. Then stitch down the large shape centrally on top, stretching it slightly.

2 Put a length of purl onto the needle and couching thread. Stitch the purl diagonally across the center of the felt from A to B, keeping a firm but even tension. Cut each purl carefully to size so that they lie neatly next to each other and continue stitching them in place, working from the center outwards.

Couched Pearl Purl

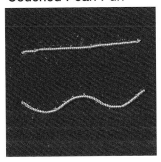

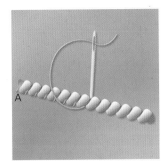

Only pearl purl, with its larger coil, can be couched in this way. Cut a length to fit along the design line and stretch it very slightly until the coils begin to separate.

Couch it in place, starting at A, using a matching couching thread and pulling the stitches firmly so that they drop down into the spiral.

Couched Twist

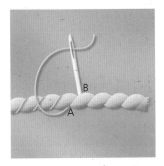

Twisted cords of varying thickness can be sewn down invisibly using a matching couching thread. Work the couching stitches diagonally from A to B, following the direction of the twist and plunge the cut ends.

Bokhara Couching

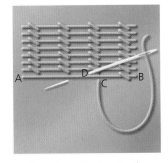

Any flexible metallic thread can be used for this solid filling. Make a long, loose stitch from A to B. Couch it down with short, regularly spaced diagonal stitches, coming up at C, going down at D and continuing to the end of the line. Couch the next line down directly below. The couching stitches can be arranged in diagonal or vertical rows.

Or Nué

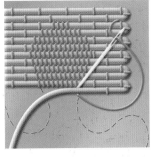

This variation of solid couching can be used to create intricate shapes made up of colored couching stitches; its name translates as "shaded gold". Draw the outline of the shape onto the fabric.

Start couching a single metallic thread with a matching couching thread.

When each line of metallic thread passes over the shape, change to a contrasting couching thread and work the stitches more closely together – the closer they are, the darker the shape will appear.

Basket Couching

This textured stitch gives an illusion of great depth. Start by couching down a foundation of string or (as here) coarse metal thread lengths, leaving small gaps between them.

Couch a single gold thread at right angles from A to B, stitching it down over every other line, then turn it back, couching in the same spaces.

For the next two rows, couch in the alternate spaces and repeat to create a basket pattern. Plunge the ends.

How to Stitch the Evening Purse

Use all the stitches you have learned to make a glamorous sampler in the guise of a simple, but dramatic evening purse. Trim the edge with gold cord and add a pretty button for the perfect finish.

You will need

12 x 16 in (30 x 40 cm) plum-colored fabric

Tissue paper

8¼ x 11 in (21 x 28 cm) heavy muslin

Embroidery slate frame

2¼ yd (2 m) medium smooth passing No. 5 in gold

DMC metallic pearl (ART 315), 1 reel in gold (5282)

12 in (30 cm) fine bright check purl

8 in (20 cm) fine smooth purl

10 in (25 cm) fine pearl purl

Small piece of yellow craft felt

1¾ yd x ⅛ in (1.5 m x 3 mm) gold twist

DMC stranded embroidery floss, 1 skein to match the fabric

15¼ in x ⅛ in (40 cm x 3 mm) coarse gold thread

Yellow polyester sewing thread to match gold threads

Polyester sewing thread to match background fabric

Selection of needles

Beeswax

11½ x 14 in (29 x 36 cm) lining fabric

9½ x 12 in (24 x 31 cm) batting

1 gold button

Preparing the fabric

1 Fold the plum fabric in half lengthwise, press lightly along the crease, then unfold.

2 Trim the corners of the muslin into curves, then fold it in half lengthwise and press to mark the center line as above. Unfold, then baste centrally to the back of the plum fabric, so that the two creases line up. The muslin will support the fine fabric and provide a structure for the bag.

3 Transfer the design on page 100 using tissue paper (page 8) centrally onto one half of the fabric, so that the bottom of the design lies along the fold. Mount the fabric on a slate frame.

Stitching the design

1 Stitch the design following the stitch diagram and key on page 100. Make sure you use three strands of embroidery floss whenever it is required and always strengthen the couching threads with wax before stitching with them.

Making the purse

1 Remove the embroidery from the frame and trim the plum fabric to within ½ in (15 mm) all around of the muslin. Turn the surplus fabric to the back over the edges of the muslin and baste it down close to the fold, taking care that the curved corners are neat.

2 Baste the lining fabric to the batting. Quilt the two layers together with parallel rows of machine stitching, worked diagonally ¾ in (2 cm) apart in both directions, to form a diamond pattern. Trim the lining fabric to within ⅜ in (1 cm) of the batting. Baste down a ⅜ in (1 cm) allowance all around.

3 With wrong sides together, place the lining onto the main bag and slipstitch the two together. Fold the bag in half, linings facing, and slipstitch the sides together, continuing along the top edge from each corner for 1⅛ in (3 cm) and leaving the rest of the top edge open.

4 Finish by slipstitching the remaining gold twist around the edge of the purse, looping it at the center of the top edge to make a button loop. Sew the button in place on the opposite side of the opening.

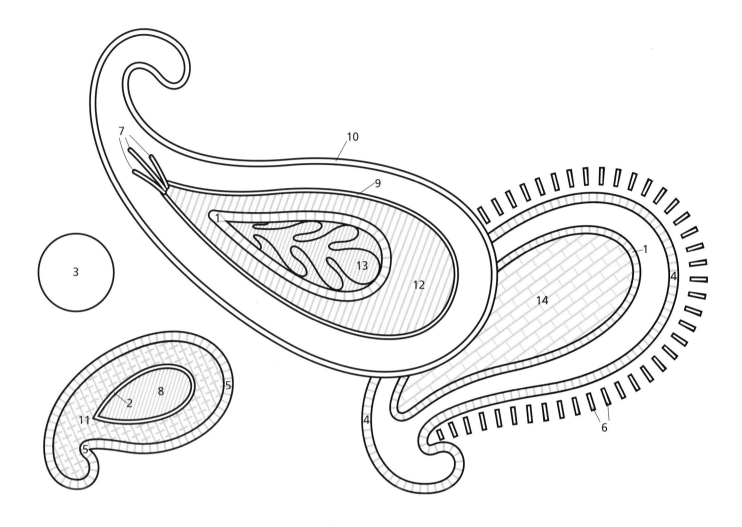

Metallic thread evening purse stitch diagram, actual size

Key

1 Double thread couching in smooth passing with yellow sewing thread

2 Single couching in smooth passing with yellow sewing thread

3 Spiral couching in smooth passing with sewing thread to match fabric

4 Open chain couching in gold metallic pearl (5282) with coton à broder

5 Blanket stitch couching in gold metallic pearl (5282) with coton à broder

6 Check purls

7 Smooth purls

8 Padded smooth purl

9 Couched pearl purl

10 Couched gold twist with yellow sewing thread

11 Burden stitch (page 76) in gold metallic pearl (5282) with coton à broder

12 Bokhara couching in gold metallic pearl (5282) with coton à broder

13 Or nué in smooth passing with sewing thread to match fabric and coton à broder

14 Basket couching in coarse gold thread and smooth passing with sewing thread to match fabric

Cutwork

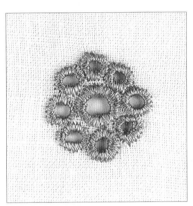

Cutwork

Cutwork has several historic variations, which have evolved over the centuries in countries from Europe to the Far East, and the term "cutwork" includes Madeira work, Irish work, Ayrshire work, Richelieu work and eyelet embroidery. They are all delicate, open styles of embroidery, featuring pierced and cut eyelets combined with outline, satin and other surface stitches. Traditionally much cutwork has been stitched in white-on-white, but the use of colored threads or background fabrics gives an interesting and contemporary look to a traditional way of working.

Round or oval eyelets arranged in a circle naturally suggest flower petals, and cutwork designs have always been predominantly pretty and floral. Larger open shapes, such as leaves, are strengthened with either a single buttonhole bar or a network of them. The designs look delicate, but the strong overcasting and buttonhole stitches mean that the fabric will stand up to repeated washing, and cutwork has long been a favorite choice for baby clothes and household linen.

FABRICS
Use a closely woven fabric that will not fray readily when cut and that will retain the shape of a pierced hole. This can be a lightweight cotton lawn, cambric, muslin or linen, depending on the fineness of the work. The fabric need not be white: a colored background with white stitching can be very effective.

THREADS
The thickness of the thread being used will vary according to the density of the design. The finest patterns can be worked in sewing thread or two strands of embroidery floss, and bolder designs in fine pearl cotton or three or more strands of embroidery floss.

NEEDLES
Choose a sharp-pointed embroidery needle that will accommodate the chosen thread and pass easily through the fabric: the length of needle is a matter of personal preference.

OTHER TOOLS
A sharp metal stiletto is used to pierce the holes for small eyelets. These can be bought from specialized suppliers, but antique examples survive and can still be used. For larger eyelets, the fabric is cut, overcast and then trimmed as necessary. Sharp scissors are vital for accurate cutting: short-bladed embroidery scissors are designed for this type of task, but curved manicure scissors can also be useful.

USES
Cutwork has been used to decorate every type of household linen from traycloths, tablecloths and napkins to pillowcases and sheets. It is also a favorite edging for trimming garments as well as for applying to cuffs and collars.

Getting started

First mount the fabric in a bound embroidery hoop (page 6) so that you can work stitches of regular length and the fabric is kept taut even when parts are cut away.

As ever when working on fine fabrics, it is important to have clean hands and to wrap the work in an old pillowcase or large handkerchief when it is not being stitched.

Preparing for stitches

To work eyelets: Outline the areas of the design that are to be cut away with small running stitches. Work these with only small spaces between them, so that most of the thread sits on the surface of the fabric. Then either overcast these areas with small, straight stitches or work buttonhole stitch (page 41) around them. Whichever technique is used, the stitches should all be the same length and spaced close together, without overlapping.

To work large open shapes: Round and oval shapes, up to

¾ in (2 cm) long and ⅜ in (1 cm) across can be worked as for the cut eyelets, but some forms of cutwork include larger open areas. Work running stitch around the outline as usual. Then work any reinforcing bars across the shape so that the ends of the bars will eventually be concealed. Finally border the shape with buttonhole stitch, so that the ridged edge lies along the inside of the shape. Carefully cut away the fabric inside the shape when the stitching is complete.

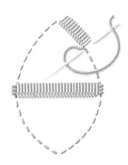

Working buttonhole stitch around a large shape before cutting away the fabric

How to make cutwork stitches

Stiletto Eyelet

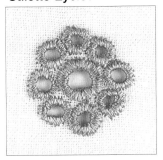

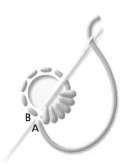

Use this technique for making small eyelets up to ⅓ in (8 mm) in diameter. Mark a circle on the fabric and work running stitches around the circumference. Pierce the fabric at the center of the circle, pushing the stiletto down until the hole is the required size. Overcast the edges of the circle with short straight stitches. Bring the needle up at A, just outside the running stitches. Take the needle back through the hole and come up at B, close to A. Continue until the circle is complete.

Buttonhole Eyelet

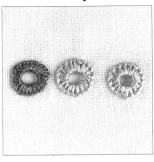

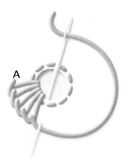

Buttonhole stitch (see page 41) can be used around a stiletto or a cut hole over the running stitches, to cover the raw edge. Bring the needle up at A, just outside the running stitches. Take the needle down through the hole and come up again close to A to make the first buttonhole stitch. Continue until the circle is complete.

The following type of embroidery may also be used with cutwork:

Free embroidery (pages 26-49)

Cut Eyelet

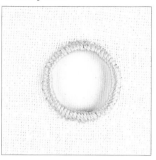

The centers of holes up to ½ in (12 mm) across and smaller petals or leaves should be clipped and turned to the wrong side before stitching. First outline the shape with running stitch. Then, using sharp small-bladed scissors, make two cuts at right angles

across the center of the surplus fabric. Turn the cut fabric back so that the fold lies alongside the running stitches and then overcast or buttonhole stitch (page 41) around the eyelet. Trim any excess fabric carefully from the wrong side.

Padded Satin Stitch

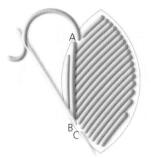

1 This raised satin stitch is traditionally used in eyelet embroidery. Stitching just within the outline, work two layers of satin stitch, the first

diagonally and the second vertically across the shape. Bring the needle up at A and make a stitch to the other side of the outline at B.

Come up again at C to make the next stitch and repeat to cover the shape. These stitches will not be visible on the back.

2 Finally, work horizontal satin stitch across the shape. Bring the needle up at A and make a stitch to B, immediately below the last stitch. Come up again at C, ready to make the next stitch. Repeat to cover the shape.

Buttonhole Bar

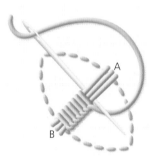

These bars add support to larger circles and petals, and are worked before the surplus fabric is cut away. First outline the shape with running stitch. Starting on the right, make a foundation for the bar of three satin stitches (page 30) across the

widest part of the shape, from A to B.
Work a row of buttonhole stitch (page 41) over the foundation from left to right: the stitches should be flat and even. Finish off neatly on the wrong side where the stitches will be covered.

Branched Buttonhole Bar

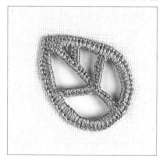

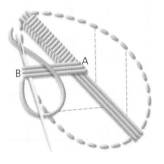

Bigger shapes need a network of bars to give them stability, and branched bars are especially good to add detail to leaves. First draw the positions for the bars on the fabric and work running stitch around the main outline. Work buttonhole stitch as for an ordinary bar, but when you reach the first branch bar at A, take the thread across to B and make another foundation bar as

before. Starting from the outside edge, buttonhole back down to the center. Continue along the central bar and work the subsequent branch bars in turn.

Loop Picot

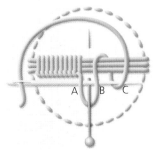

These delicate loops decorate bars and are secured with a buttonhole stitch (page 41).

Work buttonhole stitch halfway across the bar and insert a pin under the bar at that point. Take the working thread below the pin and then pass the needle over and under the bar. Slip the needle under the working thread at A, over the pin, under the thread at B, and over and under the thread at C. Gently pull the thread through so this stitch lies close to the others. Remove the pin and complete the bar. To work a double picot, space the first row of buttonholes a little wider and work a second row on the other side of the bar, sewing between the stitches. Work the two picots opposite each other so they are both central to the bar.

Scalloped Edge

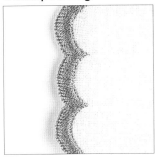

Work a row of running stitches to mark the curved edge of the shape. Add a few more parallel rows of running stitches if a padded effect is required. Then buttonhole along the edge, keeping all the stitches the same length. When complete, trim the surplus fabric close to the stitches.

Cutwork brooch cushion stitch diagram: set photocopier to 111% to copy image to correct size for the embroidery

How to Stitch the Brooch Cushion

Small decorative cushions were popular accessories for Victorian ladies, who used them to display their favorite brooches on their dressing tables. The "broderie anglaise"-style embroidery here is very fine, worked in sewing thread on white lawn, but thicker thread on heavier fabric would be just as effective.

You will need
12 x 28 in (30 x 70 cm) white lawn or
    other cotton fabric
Embroidery frame
Sewing or Danish flower thread,
    1 skein of each of the following
    colors:
Pale lemon
Spring green
Light blue
Sugar pink
White sewing thread
Toy stuffing

Key

 Pale yellow

 Spring green

Light blue

 Sugar pink

 Stiletto eyelet

Buttonhole eyelet

 Cut eyelet

Padded satin stitch

Buttonhole bar

Loop picot

Scalloped edge

 Stem stitch

Preparing the fabric
1 Cut a 8 x 12 in (20 x 30 cm) rectangle of fabric.
2 Enlarge and transfer the design on page 105, including the scallop edges and the dotted lines, onto the fabric.
3 Mount the fabric in an embroidery frame (page 6).

Working the design
1 Work the flowers and eyelets following the stitch diagram on page 105. Then work the rest of the surface stitchery. Finally work the scalloped edges.
2 Remove the fabric from the frame. Trim the scalloped edges and cut the fabric along the lines as shown on the diagram.

Making the cushion
1 Cut two 5¼ in (13 cm) squares from the remaining fabric.
2 Press under and stitch a narrow double hem along one edge of both squares. Press under a ⅜ in (1 cm) allowance on the opposite side of each square.
3 With right sides together, pin and baste the two squares to the cushion front so that the raw edges match, the folded edges align with the base of the scallops, and the hemmed edges overlap each other. Machine stitch the top and bottom seams, making a ⅜ in (1 cm) seam allowance.
4 Turn right sides out and hand sew the folded edges in place along the base of the scallops with tiny stitches.
5 To make the cushion pad, cut a 8 x 9½ in (20 x 24 cm) rectangle from the remaining fabric. Press in half widthwise. Pin, baste and machine stitch around the three open edges, leaving a 1½ in (4 cm) gap in the center of one edge. Turn right side out. Lightly fill with the pad with stuffing and slipstitch to close the gap. Insert the pad into the cushion cover.

Drawn Thread Work

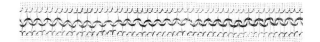

Drawn thread work is a literal description of how a fabric is prepared to produce an area on which the stitches are worked. Threads can be pulled horizontally, vertically or both. If the threads are pulled horizontally, a band of vertical threads (it can be any depth) is left and stitches are worked on regular groups of these: this is the most common method used in conjunction with a hem. Vertical drawn threads similarly produce a vertical band. Threads drawn in both directions produce a combination of bands of threads and open squares, useful for decorating square pieces such as napkins and pillowcases. Most of the stitches are variations of hemstitch, but needleweaving can also be used for more elaborate work.

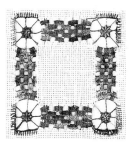

FABRICS
The stitches are usually worked on evenweave fabric such as linen — the finer the weave, the more intricate the work. Traditionally this would have been white, but now a wonderful range of colors is available. Pastel colors are best so that the fine stitchery is not overwhelmed by the fabric.

THREADS
Use stranded embroidery floss or fine pearl cotton. Again the classic drawn thread work was done with white thread on white fabric — any combination of colors can be used, but this is a delicate form of embroidery where the pattern of holes created between the threads is as important as the stitches themselves, so it is better not to have too dominant a color for the stitching.

NEEDLES
Use blunt-ended tapestry needles.

USES
Drawn thread work makes a subtle embellishment for all types of household linen including tablecloths and napkins, sheets and pillowcases. It is also particularly suitable for delicate clothes and accessories, such as camisole tops, nightdresses, babies' christening gowns and linen handkerchiefs.

Preparing the fabric

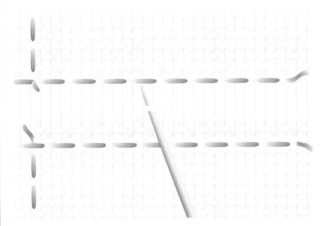

To draw threads for a border: Mark the top and bottom edges of the border with basting threads, stitching between two weft (horizontal) threads. Mark the vertical center. With a small pair of scissors, cut the horizontal threads at the center being careful not to cut any vertical threads. Withdraw the horizontal threads completely using a tapestry needle.

To draw threads for a panel: Work as for the border, but also mark the start and finish of the panel with basting threads, to give the exact number of vertical threads required. Darn the withdrawn threads a short distance into the fabric at either end of the panel and trim off the excess. Alternatively, cut off the threads and buttonhole the edges.

How to make drawn thread stitches

Single Hem Stitch

The following types of embroidery may also be used on drawn threads:
Hardanger (pages 122-4)
Cutwork (pages 102-107)

1 On the left-hand side, make a couple of stitches to secure the thread. Insert the needle two horizontal threads down from the drawn border and bring out two (or four) vertical threads along in the drawn border.

2 Reinsert the needle two (or four) threads to the left of where it emerged and bring out at the right of this group of threads. Insert the needle two horizontal threads immediately below, ready to start the next stitch.

Single Hem Stitch, alternative method

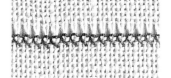

1 On the left-hand side, make two stitches below the starting point to secure the thread. Take the needle four vertical threads to the right and insert behind these threads.

2 Bring the needle through to the front, reinsert to the right of the group of vertical threads and bring out again three horizontal threads directly below this point. Pull up the thread to make a bundle of threads and repeat.

Ladder Stitch

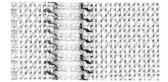

Work single hem stitch along one edge of the panel or border, then repeat along the opposite edge, being careful to work on the same groups of threads. This forms the basis of the combination stitches below.

Serpentine Stitch

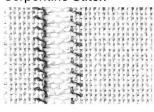

A variation of ladder stitch. Work as for ladder stitch, but when working the opposite edge, move one or two threads to the left (i.e. half the number of threads in the grouping on the first side), to form a zigzag effect.

Single Twist Stitch

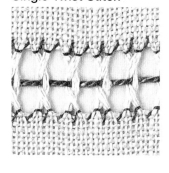

Work a ladder stitch panel or border. The number of vertical threads should be a multiple of six or eight. Take the needle up to the middle of the panel on the right, insert the needle from left to right under the second group of threads from the starting point, then under the first group. Repeat, pulling the thread taut as you do so, thereby twisting the threads.

Double Twist Stitch

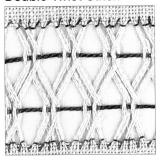

Work as for single twist stitch in the bottom half of the drawn thread panel, then turn the work upside down and repeat in the upper half, but leave the first group of threads free, so that the twists are staggered.

Coral Cluster Stitch

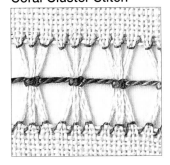

Work a ladder stitch panel or border. The number of vertical threads should be a multiple of nine. Take the needle up to the middle of the panel on the right, insert under three groups of vertical threads, bringing the needle to the front through

the middle of the loop to form a knot. Continue to the end of the row.

Lattice Border Stitch

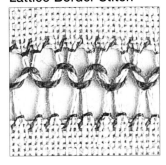

Work a ladder stitch panel or border. The number of vertical threads should be a multiple of four or six. Take the needle a third of the way up the panel to the left, encircle two groups of vertical threads from the front. Move the needle two

thirds of the way up the panel and encircle the next two vertical groups. Move down to the original level and repeat to the end of the row.

Double Knotted Lattice

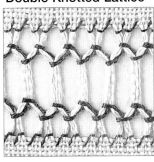

Work a ladder stitch panel or border. The number of vertical threads should be a multiple of four or six. Take the needle up four horizontal threads on the left, encircle two groups of vertical threads from behind to form a knotted loop.

Move the needle to the right and repeat, but at a slightly higher level. Continue to the end of the row, then turn the work upside down and repeat, being careful to select the same groups of threads.

Italian Hem Stitch

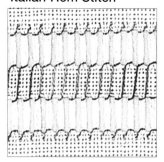

A two-layered hem stitch. Withdraw threads to make two panels with an

unworked band between. This can be any depth, in the diagram it is the same depth as the drawn thread bands. Work single hem stitch along the top edge of the upper panel and the bottom edge of the lower panel. Take the needle to the top right of the unworked band, encircle the group of thread formed by the hem

stitch from left to right, then take the needle vertically down in front of the work to the bottom of the unworked panel. Encircle a group of threads as before and take the needle up at the back of the work to the right of the next group of threads in the upper panel.

Ribbed Wheel

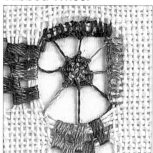

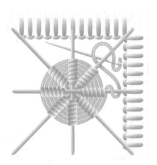

This is a filler stitch for the open corners formed when threads are drawn in a

square. Work buttonhole stitch around the two outer sides of the corner. Work an 8-barred cross from corner to corner, then take the needle to the center of the cross. Working counterclockwise, wrap the thread around each bar from under to over, then take the needle underneath the next bar and repeat. Continue in this way until

the circle has reached the desired size, then take the needle to the edge and fasten off.

Needleweaving

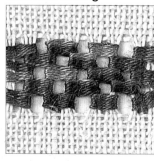

Bring the needle to the front at the bottom right of the panel, take to the back 3 or 4 threads to the

left. Bring out again 3 or 4 threads to the left and take a back stitch to the middle of the group just made. Take the needle to the right behind the next 3 or 4 threads and repeat until the weaving reaches halfway up the drawn thread panel. Finish by bringing the needle to the front halfway through the group of threads and

begin the needleweaving again, this time moving 3 or 4 threads to the left and working to the top of the drawn thread panel.

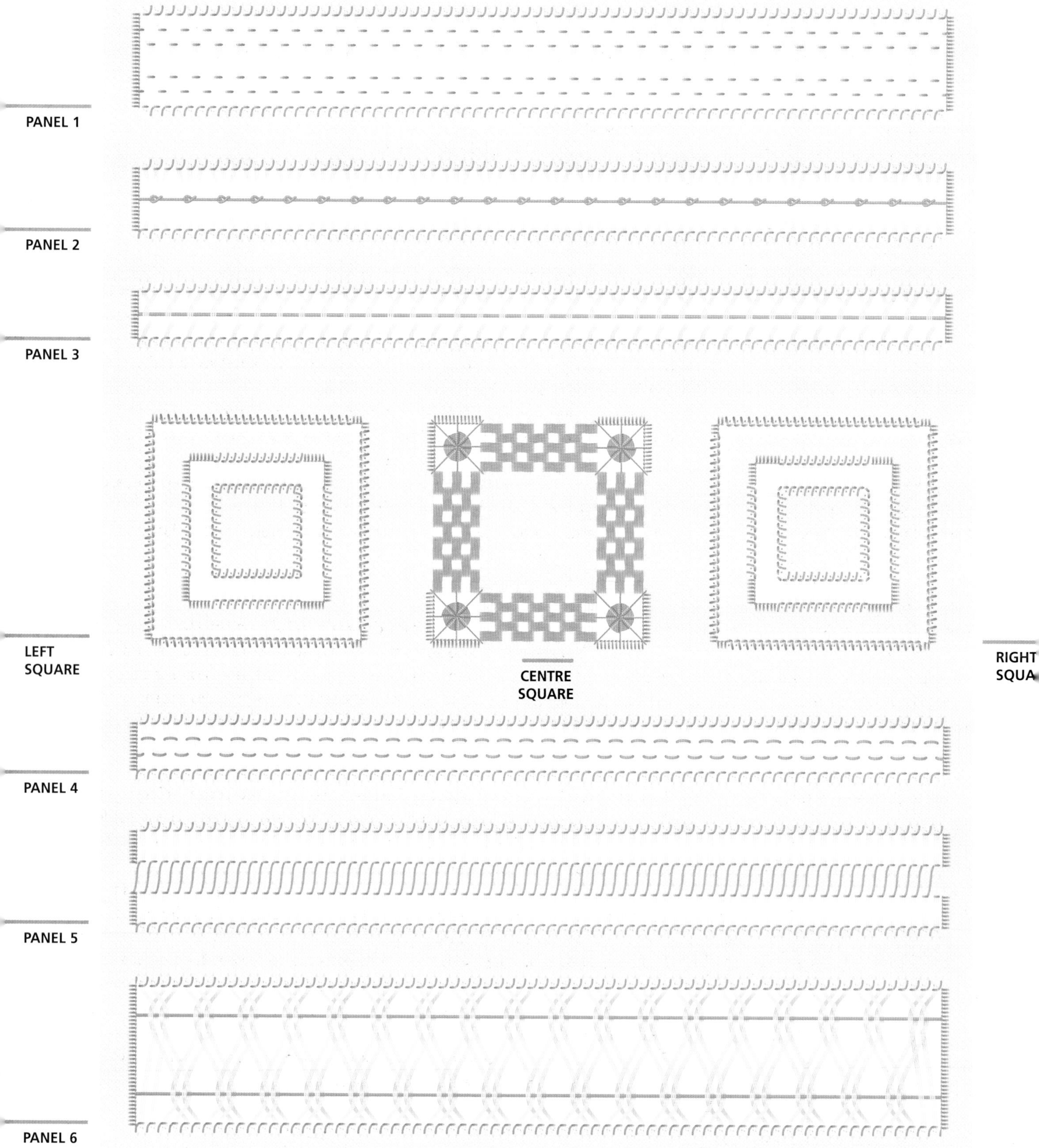

PANEL 1

PANEL 2

PANEL 3

LEFT SQUARE

CENTRE SQUARE

RIGHT SQUA

PANEL 4

PANEL 5

PANEL 6

How to Stitch the Drawn Thread Sampler

This distinctive sampler has been stitched with a variegated thread to give an unusual effect. In the central square, needle-weaving stitches show how different stitches can be introduced.

You will need

16½ x 18 in (42 cm x 46 cm) pale blue
    28-count linen
Small embroidery scissors
DMC stranded embroidery floss,
    1 skein of graded blue (121)
DMC coton perlé No. 5, 1 skein of
    graded blue (121)
Size 26 tapestry needle
Heavy white cardboard to fit picture
frame
Picture frame (optional)

Key

Panel 1: Double knotted lattice;
Panel 2: Coral cluster stitch;
Panel 3: Single twist stitch;
Panel 4: Lattice border stitch;
Panel 5: Italian hem stitch;
Panel 6: Double twist stitch.
Left inner square: Ladder stitch;
Left outer square: Single hem stitch,
    alternative method;
Center square: needleweaving with
    ribbed wheel corners;
Right inner square: Serpentine
    stitch;
Right outer square: Single hem
    stitch, alternative method

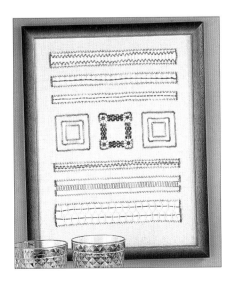

Preparing the fabric

1 Bind the edges of the fabric (page 6).
2 Find the center of the fabric, 3½ in (9 cm) down from the top edge, and mark it with a pin.

Working the first panel

1 For the first panel, cut down through 24 threads, starting at the pin. Withdraw these threads for about 3½ in (9 cm) on both sides of the center.
2 Work ladder stitch along the top and bottom edges, using a single strand of embroidery floss and stitching the fabric threads into bundles of three. If necessary, withdraw more threads at each end of the panel so that there are exactly 72 bundles in all.
3 Using a single strand of embroidery floss, work buttonhole stitch over three fabric threads, at each end of the panel. Clip the ends of the drawn fabric threads close to the buttonhole stitch.
4 Work a row of basting stitches down from each end of the first panel so that all the other panels will be exactly the same width.
5 Using three strands of embroidery floss, work double knotted lattice across the first panel.

Working panels two to six

1 Following the chart opposite, work down the fabric, withdrawing threads as indicated and working the stitches over the number of vertical threads shown. Use a single strand of embroidery floss to work the hem stitches and the buttonhole stitched edges. Use three strands of embroidery floss to work the stitches across the panels.

Working the squares

1 Baste three 2 in (5 cm) squares, equally spaced, in the center of the gap.
2 For the two outer squares, withdraw two fabric threads along the outside edges so that each side is exactly 56 threads wide. Work these areas as shown on the stitch diagram.
3 To make the inner squares, leave eight fabric threads in place and then withdraw six threads. Hemstitch around the outer edge. Work the inner rows as shown on the stitch diagram.
4 For the central square, withdraw 12 threads on each side. Buttonhole stitch around the corners and trim the drawn fabric threads. Needleweave across the drawn threads on each side of the square using a single strand of embroidery floss.
5 Use coton perlé No. 5 to make eight spokes across each corner of the square. Work a ribbed wheel stitch in the center.

Mounting the sampler

1 Place the linen right side down on a clean towel and carefully press.
2 Place the card centrally on top of the wrong side of the sampler. Lace the linen over the card (page 8). Fit in a frame of your choice.

Pulled Fabric Work

The object of pulled fabric work is to form a decorative finish by distorting the threads in the fabric with a variety of stitches. As none of the fabric threads are removed during stitching, the finished work is just as strong and durable as the original fabric. The technique involves pulling most of the embroidery stitches as tight as possible, which makes it an ideal form of decorative stitching for the novice to attempt because there are no potential problems with tricky stitch tensions.

FABRICS

This form of stitching is best worked on an evenweave fabric, which could be pure cotton or a cotton and linen or rayon mix. These fabrics are strong and able to withstand the distortion of the fabric threads. Traditionally white or cream fabric was used with the decorative stitching in the same shade. However, with modern colored fabrics, a little experimentation can produce stunning results.

THREADS

Pearl cotton is particularly suitable for this type of work because it is strong and available in four different thicknesses. Stranded embroidery floss is also suitable and encourages experimentation with the number of strands used for each element of the stitching. Traditionally the color of thread was selected to match the fabric, but the huge range of different threads and shades that are now available can produce unique and unusual results. For example, a little gold thread used sparingly in a piece of work can produce beautiful results.

NEEDLES

Always use a blunt-ended tapestry needle. Choose either No. 26 for finer threads and fabric or No. 24 as a good general-purpose needle.

USES

Pulled fabric work is strong and durable, making it particularly suitable for anything that needs to be regularly laundered. Table, bed and bathroom linen provide plenty scope for practical applications. Pulled fabric work is also lovely for the less practical items such as lavender bags, potpourri sachets, needle cases and even handmade greeting cards.

Preparing the fabric

Bind the edges of the fabric to prevent it from fraying (page 6).
Always use a suitable embroidery hoop or frame to give even support to the ground fabric during stitching. All pulled thread stitches are worked under high tension. Pull each stitch very tight so that it distorts the threads in the fabric and produces the desired decorative effect.

Starting and finishing

To start an area of stitching, leave a length of thread at the back of the work to finish off later. Secure the loose ends of thread by weaving them into the back of stitches.

How to make pulled thread stitches

Satin Stitch

Satin stitch is often used to outline and define the borders of a piece of pulled fabric work. Bring the needle up at one end of the lower edge of the shape to be filled. Make a straight, vertical stitch to the top of

the shape. Pull the thread through until it just sits smoothly on the surface of the fabric. Bring the needle up again one fabric thread to the left and continue making stitches until the shape is complete.

Eyelet Stitch

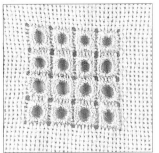 

This stitch creates a small hole in the center of a square, in this case covering six fabric threads in each direction. One eyelet can be worked on its own, or eyelets can be repeated to make a filling. Bring the needle up on the outer edge of the

square and make a stitch over three fabric threads into the central point. Pull the thread very tight and make the next stitch in the same way, but starting from the next hole around the square. Work seven stitches on each side of the square.

Diagonal Satin Stitch

 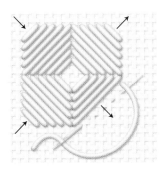

For this stitch, satin stitches are worked diagonally to make a textured pattern of alternating squares. Work nine satin stitches over six fabric threads to make the first square, making the stitches from right to left and

drawing each one very tight. Bring the needle up again two intersections diagonally to the right and make the second square, working the stitches from left to right in the same direction as those for the first square.

Fill in the remaining two squares in the same way, but working the stitches along the opposite diagonal and using shared holes on the inner edges of the squares. Repeat the stitch to create an even filling.

The following embroidery may also be used with pulled fabric work: Drawn thread work (pages 108–115), Hardanger (pages 122–4)

Chessboard Filling Stitch

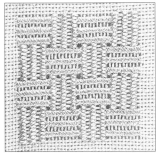 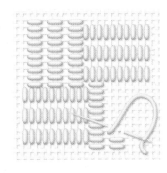

Work three upright rows of satin stitch, each row with ten stitches over three fabric threads, pulling each stitch very tight. Work the next block in the same way, but with rows of ten horizontal stitches. Complete the filling by alternating the direction of each block of stitches.

Wave Filling Stitch

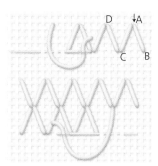

Bring the needle up at A and make a diagonal stitch to B, two fabric threads to the right and four down, drawing the thread tight. Bring the needle up again at C, four fabric threads to the left, and make a diagonal

stitch back to A. Bring the needle up again at D, four fabric threads to the left, ready to repeat the sequence and complete the row. Work subsequent rows underneath to create a diamond filling.

Ringed Back Stitch

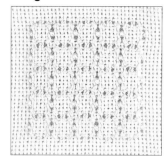

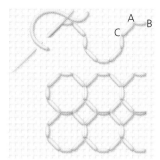

Bring the needle up at A and make a back stitch to B, two fabric threads to the right, pulling the stitch tight. Come up again two intersections down to the left of A, at C and make a back stitch to A. Continue to backstitch in a

semicircular pattern. Then complete the rings by backstitching back across the row. On the second row of rings, work a second stitch where the rings touch.

Three-sided Stitch

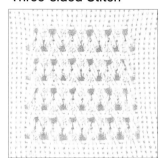

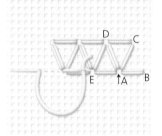

This stitch can be worked horizontally, vertically or in closely packed rows. Bring the needle up at A and make a back stitch to B, four fabric threads to the right. Repeat the same stitch, pulling the thread tight. Come up again at A and make a stitch diagonally up to C, two fabric threads to the right and four up. Repeat the

same stitch, pulling the thread tight. Now come up at D, four fabric threads to the left and make a stitch back to C. Repeat the stitch as before. Come up again at D, make a stitch to A and then repeat that stitch. Come up at D, four threads to the left and repeat the sequence.

Punch Stitch

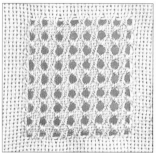

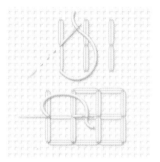

1 Bring the needle up and make a straight stitch upwards over four fabric threads. Repeat the same stitch, pulling the thread tight. Now come up four fabric threads down to the left and repeat the two stitches in the same way. Continue working this pattern in rows to fill the area.

2 To complete, turn the work 90 degrees and work double stitches in the same way, using the same holes as the previous stitches.

Ridge Stitch

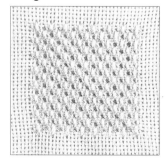

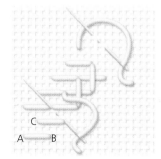

This stitch is pulled as tight as possible to form raised diagonal ridges. Bring the needle up at A and make a stitch to B, four fabric threads to the right. Come up at C, two fabric threads diagonally up to the left, ready to make the next stitch in the same

way. Complete a diagonal line of horizontal stitches. Work back along the same row making vertical stitches, each one from the end of the previous horizontal stitch, over four threads, to the opposite end of the next horizontal stitch.

Net Filling

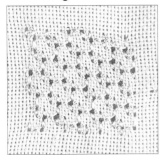

Start at the top right and bring the needle up at A, three fabric threads below. Make a stitch to B, pulling the thread tight. Come up at C, three intersections down to the left and make a stitch to A. Come up at D, three intersections to the left, ready to repeat the sequence and complete the row. Turn the work over and run the needle back to the starting point under the stitches, taking care that the trailing thread does not show through the holes.

To start the next row, bring the needle up at C and make a stitch to E, over two fabric threads. Come up at F, two intersections to the left, and make a stitch to C. Repeat the same pattern of stitches in relation to the first row. To complete the pattern, make a mirror image of the stitches on the previous row to form small squares. Start the next row, to repeat the whole pattern, at X.

Coil Stitch Filling

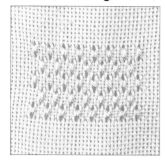

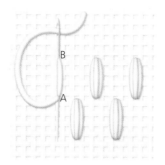

Bring the needle up at A and make a straight stitch up over four fabric threads to B. Repeat the stitch from A to B twice more. Then come up four fabric threads to the left and repeat the sequence to the end of the row. To work the next row, position the top of each triple stitch on the same line as the base of the previous row and centered between two triple stitches.

Lavender bag chart: enlarge on a photocopier for ease of working

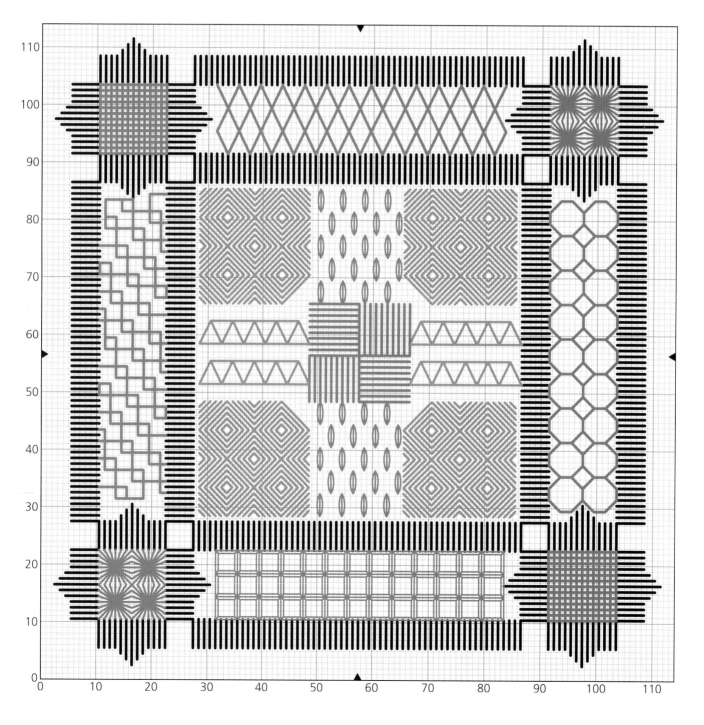

How to Stitch the Lavender Bag and Sachet

These traditional pulled fabric stitches are perfect – they allow the soothing fragrance of lavender to escape from this little bag and sachet, to mingle with your favorite linen.

You will need

For the lavender bag:

10¼ x 5¼ in (26 x 13.5 cm) ivory 27-count Linda fabric

DMC coton perlé in No. 5, 8 and 12, 1 x 10 g ball of each in ivory

½ yd (50 cm) narrow cream ribbon

For the lavender sachet:

6¾ x 7¾ in (17 x 19.5 cm) ivory 27-count Linda fabric

DMC coton perlé No. 8, 1 x 10g ball in ivory

Small quantity of dried lavender

For both projects:

Blunt-ended tapestry needle

Embroidery frame or hoop

Key

Note: one grid line represents one fabric thread

◉ Plain satin stitch in coton perlé No. 5

▦ Ridge stitch in coton perlé No. 8

▢ Punch stitch in coton perlé No. 8

▩ Wave stitch in coton perlé No. 8

❀ Net filling in coton perlé No. 8

▬ Diagonal satin stitch in coton perlé No. 12

⁝⁝ Coil stitch in coton perlé No. 8

▬ Chessboard filling in coton perlé No. 8

⌇⌇ Three-sided stitch in coton perlé No. 12

∞ Ringed back stitch in coton perlé No. 8

▪ Eyelet in coton perlé No. 8

Preparing the fabric

1 For either project, bind the edges of the fabric. It may be easier to work on a larger piece of fabric, trimming it down after working the decorative stitches and then finishing the edges to prevent them from fraying. Baste the given fabric dimensions onto it to give you the decorative stitching area.

2 For the lavender bag, measure 3 in (7.5 cm) down from the short top edge and 2½ in (6.5 cm) in from long edge. Baste two short lines where these points cross, which is the exact center point of the design.

3 For the lavender sachet, measure ⅜ in (1 cm) in from both edges. Baste two short lines where these points cross, which gives you the corner starting point for stitching.

4 For either project, mount the fabric on an embroidery frame or hoop.

Stitching the lavender bag

1 Stitch all the plain satin stitches first, counting them very carefully following the chart and the key.

2 Next work all the decorative stitching in the outer border.

3 To complete the embroidery, stitch the central panel.

Making the lavender bag

1 Fold the fabric in half, aligning the short edges and with wrong sides together.

2 Stitch two side seams, ⅜ in (1 cm) outside the embroidered area. Stitch one seam all the way along, but stop ¾ in (2 cm) from the top of the second seam to allow for feeding through the ribbon.

3 Fold the top edge over by ⅜ in (1 cm) and then fold over the same again. Stitch the hem neatly in place.

4 Turn the bag right side out and feed ribbon through the top hem. Cut the ends of ribbon at an angle to prevent fraying, leaving them loose so you can use the ribbon to tie the bag onto a clothesrod in your closet.

Stitching the lavender sachet

1 Using coton perlé No. 8 and starting in one corner, stitch a 3 in (7.5 cm) square of chessboard filling with nine chessboard squares along each edge.

Making the lavender sachet

1 Fold the fabric in half, aligning the short edges and with wrong sides together.

2 Stitch two side seams directly along the edges of the decorative stitching.

3 Turn the sachet right sides out and fill with dried lavender.

4 Finish the sachet by turning in and overcast the open edges together; place it inside the bag.

Hardanger

Originating on the west coast of Norway, Hardanger combines many disciplines of needlecraft. Fabric threads bounded by Kloster blocks of satin stitches are cut and removed to form a delicate meshwork on which needlelace and needle weaving are worked. The uncut areas of fabric are embellished with surface embroidery as simple or as elaborate as the stitcher wishes.

FABRICS

Hardanger is best worked on pure cotton or cotton-linen mix evenweave fabric. Special Hardanger fabric is also available, but it is quite firm and only suitable for flat projects. Damask Hardanger fabric drapes beautifully, but it is quite difficult to count threads and so should only be used by the experienced stitcher. Traditionally white or cream fabrics were used, but it is worth experimenting with the many different shades now available.

THREADS

Pearl cotton is ideal for Hardanger because it is available in four thicknesses. Stranded embroidery floss is also suitable and it is well worth trying different numbers of strands to vary the effect. Traditionally the shade of thread was chosen to match the fabric. However, contrasting thread will also produce unique and attractive embroidery.

NEEDLES

Always use a blunt-ended tapestry needle. Use either a No. 24 or 26, according to preference. A No. 26 is best for finer threads and fabric, while a No. 24 is a pretty good all-rounder.

OTHER TOOLS

A small pair of very sharp-pointed embroidery scissors is essential for cutting fabric threads and a pair of tweezers to help pick out the cut threads.

USES

Hardanger is perfect for tablemats, cushion covers, tablecloths, table runners, shelf edgings, needlecases, bookmarks and book covers. As well as having these very practical uses, smaller pieces of elaborate Hardanger will also make highly decorative and beautiful framed pictures.

Preparing the fabric

Cut a piece of your chosen fabric, allowing at least 2 in (5 cm) extra all around. Bind the edges of the fabric to prevent them from fraying (page 6).

Refer to the design chart or instructions to find out where the stitching should start. Mark the start point, which may be the center, with a line of running stitches with brightly colored sewing thread. This will help you count fabric threads when you are stitching.

Always mount the fabric in an embroidery hoop or a frame (page 6), according to size and personal preference.

Starting and finishing

To start an area of stitching, leave a 3 in (8 cm) tail secured by a couple of backstitches. These can be unpicked and woven in on the reverse side later. To finish, slip the needle under a few stitches on the wrong side.

Cutting the threads

The threads are not cut until all the kloster blocks and surface embroidery have been completed. Check that the blocks are exactly opposite one another and that no threads have been skipped. If you have arrived back where you started, the stitching is likely to be accurate. Use fine pointed scissors to cut the threads.

Cutting threads on larger motifs

Check that the stitches are worked along a thread, and count each side carefully before cutting. Cut the threads in groups of four rather than trying to cut across eight or twelve threads at once.

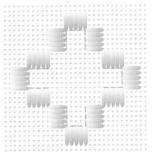

1 Only cut threads between satin stitches and not at the sides of the block, so where there are five satin stitches, the four fabric threads inbetween are cut.

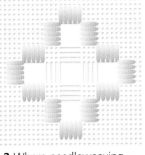

2 Where needleweaving stitches are to be worked within a motif, some of the threads are left uncut. Pull the cut threads out with tweezers to leave a grid of threads arranged in a square pattern.

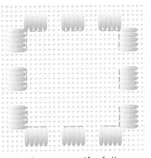

3 On larger motifs, follow the cut threads across and cut the other end on the opposite side of the motif.

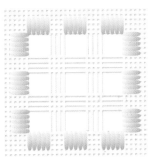

4 Work around the motif, cutting the remaining threads. Pull the cut threads out to leave a grid of threads, as shown.

How to make Hardanger stitches

Kloster blocks

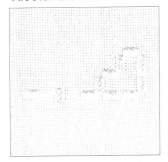

Kloster blocks are worked in a straight line to make square and rectangular motifs. The last block should touch the first.

1 Work five satin stitches over four threads. This is the basic kloster block. Take a large diagonal stitch, bringing the needle out four threads

up. Work a second block.
2 To turn a corner, on the last stitch turn the needle at right angles and bring it out four threads away.

The following embroidery may also be used with Hardanger:
Canvas work (pages 150–169)
Drawn thread work (pages 108–115)
Pulled fabric work (pages 116–121)

Wrapped bars

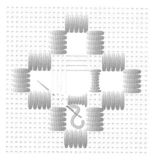

Keep your finger behind the fabric threads to tension them slightly and overcast the fabric threads quite tightly. Take the needle across the back to wrap the next bar. Work around the block and secure the thread on the reverse side.

Woven Bars

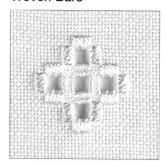

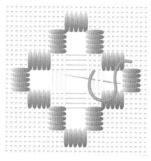

1 Bring the needle out in the middle of the group of fabric threads and take a backstitch over the first two threads.

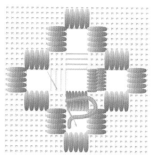

2 Weave over and under two threads, pulling the thread quite tight for each stitch. Continue weaving in a figure-eight pattern until the bar is full. Take the needle to the reverse side and bring it out in the middle of the next group of threads to be woven. Continue until all the bars are woven and sew the end in on the reverse side.

Woven bars with picots

The picot can be worked on one side only, or both as shown here.

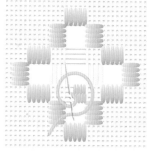

1 Weave half the way across the fabric threads and insert the needle halfway into the bar. Wrap the thread around the needle and pull the needle through to form the picot.

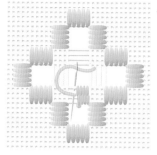

2 Weave the needle through in the opposite direction and make a picot stitch on the other side. Complete the woven bar.

Dove's eye filling (Also known as Web filling)

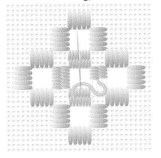

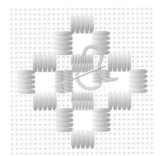

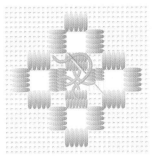

This delicate filling stitch can be worked on both woven and wrapped bars.

1 Weave or wrap three of the bars. On the last one, work halfway across the fabric threads, then take a small stitch through the center of the next bar.

2 Take the needle under the first part of the web, bringing the needle out in the middle of the next bar.

3 Take a stitch into each bar in turn until you are back where you started. Complete the weaving or wrapping on the last bar.

Lace stitch

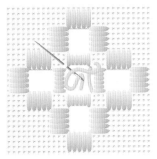

Eyelet

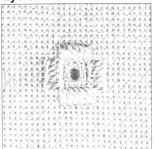

Work in the same way as for the Dove's eye filling (above), but work the stitches of the

web into the corners of the square.

Eyelets are usually worked in the center of a small square of kloster blocks using a finer thread. Work each stitch into the central hole at one end

and into the same hole as each satin stitch on the other all the way around the square. Pull the threads firmly to form a hole in the center.

Larger cutwork motifs

Larger cutwork motifs are worked with decorative satin stitch borders rather than the basic kloster block. The larger cutwork areas are filled with ornate needlelace designs.

The satin stitches can vary in length to create a variety of patterns. There has to be a specific number of stitches, so that the threads can be grouped and cut in the same way as the smaller kloster

blocks. As there is a fabric thread between each satin stitch, work one more satin stitch than the threads required on each side. The samples shown on page 126 are all based on a

12-thread square with 13 satin stitches on each side. Larger cutwork squares are based on the four times table, as the threads are cut or woven in groups or multiples of four.

Crenellated edge

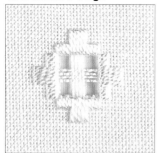

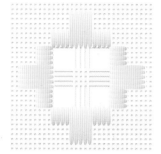

As an alternative to kloster blocks, decorative satin stitch borders can be worked. Work four satin stitches over four threads and then five stitches over eight threads,

then complete the side with four stitches over four threads again. Cut the threads in the same way as the straight edge.

Star edge

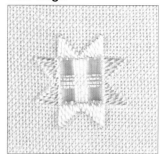

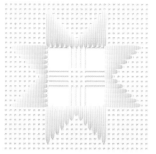

Another variation of decorative satin stitch. Work the first satin stitch over eight threads and then work each stitch over one less thread until the center stitch

is over two threads. To complete the side, work stitches of increasing length back up to the final stitch over eight threads.

Diamond edge

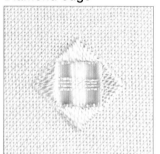

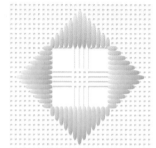

A variation of decorative satin stitch that produces a diamond shaped edging around the open square. Work the first satin stitch over two threads and then

work each stitch over one more thread until the center stitch is over eight threads. Work back down, stitching over two threads to complete the side.

Satin stitch

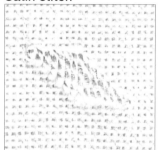

Satin stitch is a surface embroidery stitch used alongside the cutwork to give Hardanger much of its characteristic effect. It is worked horizontally, diagonally or vertically to produce a wide range of different geometric and naturalistic motifs to fill in the fabric areas around the

cutwork. The number of motifs is limitless, but some, such as the tulip and eight-pointed star, are very popular. Use the same thickness of thread as for the kloster blocks.
Work the straight stitches using an even tension in adjacent holes of the fabric.

Tulip

Count the threads carefully, working the satin stitches for the first side of the tulip and then work the second side of

the tulip, using the same holes for the threads in the center of the tulip.

Eight-pointed star

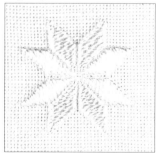

Another popular surface embroidered motif. Count the threads carefully, working the first point of the star.

Continue around the star, using the same holes for the threads that butt together.

Cable stitch

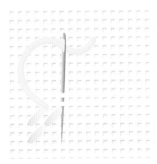

Cable stitch can be pulled slightly to draw the threads, forming tiny holes or simply stitched as a diagonal backstitch. Use a finer thread for pulled work on loose weave linens and heavier thread for a bold line. Take a stitch diagonally over two threads and then bring the needle out two threads to one side. Make another stitch diagonally and bring out at the top of the first stitch. Continue working diagonally, alternating the needle from row to row to create two parallel lines of stitches.

How to stitch the Hardanger Tablemat

The combination of Hardanger's satisfying geometry and delicate lacy patterns is a real joy, and this lovely tablemat will introduce you to the appeal of the technique.

You will need

16½ x 13¾ in (42 x 35 cm) 28-count
    Quaker cloth
Embroidery frame or large hoop
DMC coton perlé in No. 5, 8 and 12,
    1 x 10 g ball of each in white
Blunt-end tapestry needle
Sharp-pointed scissors

Preparing the fabric

1 Bind the edges of the fabric (page 6) to prevent fraying.
2 Find the center of the fabric (page 6) and mark the center of the chart with a pen.
3 Mount the fabric on the frame or in the hoop. If you choose a hoop, make sure it is large enough for the whole design area, to avoid moving the embroidery and risking damage to the white stitches.

Stitching the tablemat

1 Following the chart opposite, first stitch all the plain satin stitch motifs in coton perlé No. 5 and the eyelets in No. 12.
2 Next cut and withdraw the fabric threads, taking great care to follow the chart and cut the correct ones. However, if a thread is cut in error (and no matter how carefully it is done, this does happen!), withdraw a length of fabric thread from the edge of work and weave it back into the fabric in the place of the cut thread.
3 Now follow the chart and key to work all the bars and filling stitches, and complete the decorative stitching.
4 To finish the mat, turn a 3 in (7.5 cm) hem, mitering the corners (page 8). Neatly hand or machine stitch the hem in place.

Key

◇ Diamond edge square in coton perlé No. 5

✴ Eight pointed star in coton perlé No. 5

✴ Star edge square in coton perlé No. 5

✦ Crenellated edge square in coton perlé No. 5

⚘ Satin stitch tulip in coton perlé No. 5

☰ Woven bar with picots in coton perlé No. 8

▪ Wrapped bar in coton perlé No. 8

𝕀 Woven bar in coton perlé No. 8

= Pairs of wrapped bars in coton perlé No. 8

▥ Kloster blocks in coton perlé No. 5

✳ Eyelet in coton perlé No. 12

¤ Lace filling in coton perlé No. 8

✧ Dove's eye filling in coton perlé No. 8

Tablemat chart: enlarge on a photocopier for ease of working

Needle Weaving

Needle weaving is a method of decorating fabric that has a long history. It can be traced back, via European folk art traditions, to ancient Coptic work, and it is more allied to tapestry weaving techniques than embroidery. To create the designs, bands of weft (horizontal) threads are withdrawn from an evenweave fabric and the original warp (vertical) threads are re-worked by wrapping and interweaving them with embroidery threads to create a new textile. Although needle weaving is, by its nature, restricted to making straight lines of pattern, it can be used in an interesting and creative way to add texture and color. Once two basic techniques have been mastered, there is endless scope to produce geometric designs.

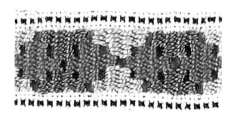

FABRICS

Evenweave fabrics, from which the threads can easily be withdrawn, should be used. Linen is ideal, although cotton can be used if a more delicate effect is required. Interesting designs can be created by working on a fabric with woven stripes or checks.

THREADS

Twisted threads, such as coton à broder, are particularly good for needle weaving and their lustrous finish contrasts well with linen. Choose a weight of thread that is slightly heavier than the background fabric to give body to the stitches. Stranded floss can be used with finer fabrics. White-on-white gives a subtle effect, but brightly colored threads give more visual impact.

NEEDLES

Use a blunt-ended tapestry needle to avoid piercing the fabric threads.

USES

The horizontal bands of pattern produced by needle weaving can be used singly or built up into intricate patterns by working parallel rows in different designs. Bands of pattern can be used to add simple geometric borders and stripes of color to any item made from an evenweave fabric, including cushion covers, napkins, tablecloths and throws.

Preparing the fabric

To draw threads for a border: Mark the top and bottom edges of the border with basting, stitching between two weft (horizontal) threads. Mark the vertical center. With a small pair of scissors, cut the weft threads at the center, taking care not to cut any warp (vertical) threads. Withdraw the weft threads completely, loosening the cut end with a tapestry needle and pulling them out from the center (see diagram page 109).

To draw threads for a panel: Mark the panel as for a border, but also mark the each end to give the exact number of warp threads required. Cut the weft threads just in the center. Withdraw the threads, but darn them a short distance into the fabric at each end of the panel. Then trim off the excess thread (see diagram page 109). Alternatively, cut off the threads and buttonhole (page 41) the edges.

Order of working: Once the threads are withdrawn, the fabric loses its structure. To minimize this effect on a design, only pull out the threads for one band at a time.

Getting started

There are two ways of covering the threads – wrapping thread around them to create a round bar and weaving thread between them to create a flat bar. All the other stitches are variations or combinations of these bars. The size of the bars can be varied by working over more or fewer threads.

Needle weaving is worked in the hand or on a frame.

To start: With the wrong side of the fabric facing you, hold the end of the working thread over the first group of warp threads and bind or weave the working thread over it. Then trim the end.

To finish: Pass the needle down through the back of the last bar, then trim the end.

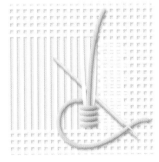

Starting

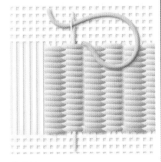

Finishing

How to make needle weaving stitches

Zigzag Clusters

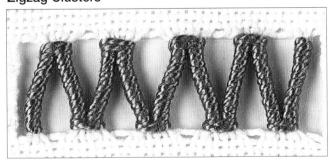

Start at A and wrap down the first group of three warp threads, wrapping the working thread from left to right. At the bottom bring the needle up three warp threads

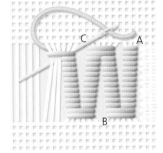

to the left, at B. Wrap the working thread twice around this and the previous group of three threads to pull them together. Then wrap the second group of three warp threads, working upwards to complete the next bar. At the top edge bring the needle up three warp threads to the left, at C. Wrap the working thread twice around the cluster to pull them together as before. Repeat this sequence to the end.

Broken Bars

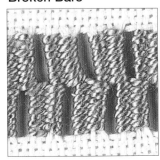

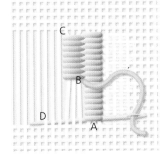

Begin by wrapping the first three warp threads from A up to the middle of the band, at B. Bring the needle out at C, three warp threads to the left. Weave over and under the first and second groups of three threads, back down to B, and covering the diagonal thread from B to C. Come up at D and weave over and under the second and third groups of threads back up to B. Continue to the end and finish by wrapping the final group of threads from the center to the edge of the band.

Bars and Clusters

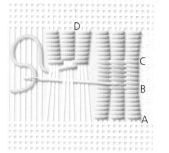

Wrap the first group of three warp threads from A to B, wrapping the working thread from left to right, to one third of the way up the band. Bring the needle up three threads to the left and wrap downwards. Then wrap upwards over the next three threads, finishing level with B. Weave under and over the three groups of threads to two-thirds up the band, coming up at C. Always wrapping the working thread from left to right, work up the first three threads, down the next three and up the final three to finish the first block. Bring the needle up three warp threads to the left, at D, to start working next block the other way up. Repeat to the end.

Diamond Blocks

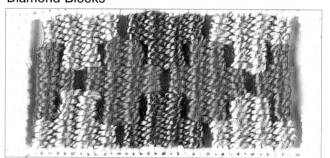

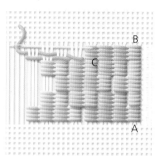

Starting at A, weave under and over four groups of three warp threads to one-fifth of the way up the band. Weave over the two center groups to two-fifths up the bar to make a pyramid shape. Take the needle up to B, work a mirror image and finish off. Bring the needle up at C, using another color. Work a diamond shape over two, four and then two groups of warp threads, incorporating two of the previous groups and two new ones. Repeat the first two blocks using a third color and then repeat the pattern to the end. Fill in the remaining spaces with half-diamond shapes. Slipstitch the needle weaving at each end of the band to the background fabric.

How to Stitch the Needle Weaving Sampler

This small sampler shows just what can be achieved with a few simple needle weaving stitches. The top and bottom edges are hemstitched, and the side edges are bound with narrow strips of the evenweave fabric. The buttons at each corner provide the finishing touch.

You will need

8 x 12 in (20 x 30 cm) 22-count
   evenweave linen or cotton
DMC coton perlé No. 5, 1 skein of
   each of the following colors:
Dark green (500)
Bright pink (602)
Pale pink (605)
Powder blue (3755)
Pale blue (3841)
Turquoise (3845)
Tapestry needle
4 x ⅝ in (15 mm) buttons

Preparing the fabric

1 Pull several threads from one long edge of the linen and reserve for the working threads and then cut out a 6 in (15 cm) square.
2 Baste under a ³⁄₁₆ in (5 mm) hem along one edge of the square. Starting ¾ in (2 cm) down from this top edge, withdraw a band of six threads. Fold the neatened edge in half and baste in place in line with the top of the withdrawn threads. Stitching with the withdrawn threads, work hemstitch (page 109) over groups of three threads.

Stitching the sampler

1 Following the diagram and key below for stitches and colors, work the first six bands of needle weaving. Leave five fabric threads between each band.
2 Withdraw six threads for the final line of zigzag clusters. Then trim the remaining fabric to 1 in (2.5 cm). Hemstitch the bottom edge as for the top edge and then work the final band of needle weaving.
3 Withdraw the center horizontal thread in each dividing block of unworked fabric and weave a length of dark green thread in its place.

Trimming the sampler

1 Cut two 1¼ x 6 in (3 x 15 cm) strips from the remaining fabric. Press under a ³⁄₁₆ in (5 mm) allowance along one long edge of each strip. Machine stitch a zigzag stitch or overcast by hand along each side edge of the finished embroidery to reinforce it.
2 With right sides together and raw edges matching, sew one strip onto each side of the embroidery with a ³⁄₁₆ in (5 mm) seam. Turn each strip to the back and fold over the short edges. Slipstitch each strip in place along the folded edge, squaring up the corners. Sew a button to each corner.

Key

Bands 1 and 7 Zigzag cluster in pale blue 3841 with 6 threads withdrawn

Bands 2 and 6 Zigzag clusters in powder blue 3755 with 7 threads withdrawn

Band 3 Broken bars in bright pink 602 with 10 threads withdrawn

Band 4 Diamond blocks with pyramids in pale blue 3841 and turquoise 3845, and diamonds in pale pink 605 with 12 threads withdrawn

Band 5 Bars and clusters in pale pink 605 with 10 threads withdrawn

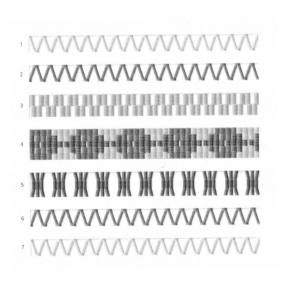

Needle weaving sampler stitch diagram: enlarge on a photocopier for ease of working

Needlelace

The poetic Italian term for this technique is *punto in aria*, which literally means "stitches in the air". This neatly sums up how it is made, as it is a branch of lacemaking rather than embroidery, and the stitches are built up in rows as a free-standing structure, instead of being sewn onto a background fabric.

Historically, needle or point lace reached the peak of fashion amid the high society of seventeenth-century Venice, where fine pieces were prized as much as precious jewels. It was time-consuming and therefore costly to make, and affordable only to the wealthy. As bobbin lace, which was relatively quicker to make, became more widely available, Venetian lace, along with the other fine points - Alençon, Argentine and Brussels - fell from favor. However, needlelace continued to be made, and there was a great revival in the nineteenth century when it was seen as a suitable recreation for ladies of leisure. Other needlelaces, including Russian or Tape lace, have remained popular and are still produced commercially in the Far East.

THREADS
Threads designed especially for lacemaking, such as *fil à dentelles* or crochet cotton, have the body required for well-formed stitches. They come in various weights – use a thicker one to start with and progress to the finer threads. Pearl cotton gives a shiny finish, but is not so easy to work with.

NEEDLES
Choose one with a blunt tip such as a fine tapestry or a ballpoint needle. The size depends on the thread being used.

USES
Tape lace can be used for small mats and other household linen. However, today needlelace is most popularly used as an important element in stumpwork and other raised embroideries.

Making a needlelace pad

Larger pieces are worked on a drum-shaped pillow, similar to that used for bobbin lace. Smaller projects and single motifs can be stitched on a simple pad. Sew three squares of muslin together to make the basic pad. Then draw the design outline onto heavy paper and baste it to the pad.
For tape lace, baste a frame of tape around the outside edge of the design outline (as in the stitch illustrations below).

Working the basic stitches

The five examples of stitches shown here are all "Point de Bruxelles" stitches, which are variations on a simple loose buttonhole stitch. The open mesh is created by building up rows of stitches from one side to the other and each row is worked into the loops made on the previous row. The various patterns are created by arranging the stitches in different formats.

1 Work the foundation row by making evenly-spaced buttonhole stitches into the top edge, starting at A and working to the right.

2 Work two small overcast stitches over the edge at B and C, and then bring the thread out at D to start the second row. Work back to the left, reversing the direction of the thread. Work the stitches in the final row through the edge of the bottom tape.

Working over a cordonnet

1 For other types of needlelace and for stumpwork, curved shapes such as petals, leaves or wings are often required. These are worked within a cordonnet – a taut loop of thread, or a fine wire when the piece needs to flex off the surface, in the shape of the motif. The shape is then completed with a round of raised buttonhole stitching, called a cordonnette (page 75).
Prepare the design outline on drawing paper and baste it to the pad. Fold a length of thread in half and, starting at the loop, couch it around the outline, spacing the stitches ⅛ in (3 mm) apart. Pass the loose ends through the loop and couch them down, too, for ¾ in (2 cm) around the outline. Trim the ends.

2 Begin the needlelace stitching with a row along the top edge of the cordonnet. As you work each following row, twist the working thread around the cordonnet at the end of each row. Secure the bottom row by working the loops around the cordonnet. Carefully snip the couching threads from the back to release the motif.

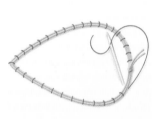

Couching the cordonnet

Working needlelace within the cordonnet

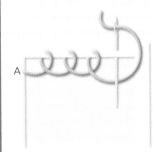

Foundation row

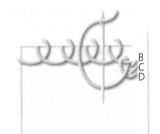

Second row

How to make needlelace stitches

Single Brussels Stitch (also known as Single Net Stitch)

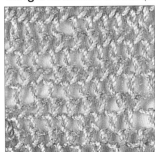

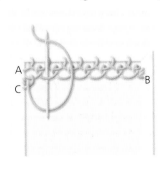

Work a foundation row of loose loops in buttonhole stitch (page 41) along the top edge of the tape (shown here) or cordonnette from the left at A to the right. Make two overcast stitches at the right edge and bring the needle out at B. Work

the return row of loops from right to left, reversing the buttonhole stitch. Repeat these two rows to fill the space.

Double Brussels Stitch (also known as Double Net Stitch)

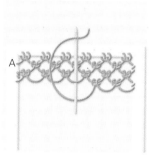

Start at A and work two buttonhole stitches next to each other from left to right. Leave a loop and work the next pair of stitches. Continue in this way to make a row of shallow loops along the top edge. Work the return row from right to left, reversing the buttonhole stitches. Repeat the two rows to fill the space.

Cloth Stitch (also known as Corded Stitch)

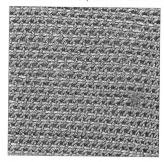

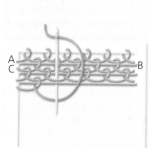

Starting at A, work a row of closely spaced buttonhole loops along the top edge. Bring the needle up at B and make a long stitch back to the left, at C. Work a second row of stitches, passing the needle behind both the loop above and the long thread. Repeat these two rows to fill the space.

Side Stitch

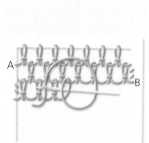

Start at A and make a loose buttonhole stitch into the top edge. Pass the needle from left to right behind the loop and over the working thread. Pull the thread through firmly to make a second buttonhole stitch across the first. Repeat at regular intervals to the right edge. Make two small overcast stitches down the right edge and come up at B. Work back along the row from right to left in the same way, reversing the stitches. Repeat the two rows to fill the space.

Pea Stitch (also known as Point de Bruxelles)

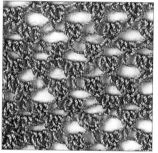

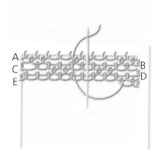

Start with a foundation of evenly spaced loops along the top edge from A. Make two overcast stitches to come out at B.
Row 2: Work a buttonhole stitch in each of the next two loops and then skip two loops. Repeat this pattern to complete the row. Make two overcast stitches to come out at C.
Row 3: Make a buttonhole stitch into the loop between the first pair of stitches, then work three buttonhole stitches into the long loop. Repeat this pattern to complete the row. Make two overcast stitches to come out at D.
Row 4: Skip two loops and then work buttonhole stitch into each of the two loops below the group of three stitches. Repeat this pattern to complete the row. Make two overcast stitches to come out at E. Repeat Rows 3 and 4 to fill the space.

How to Stitch the Needlelace Bookmark

Making this project, which is worked in spring-like shades, is a good way to become familiar with needlelace stitches. Instead of using a pad or pillow, the tape is machine stitched directly onto an acetate background, which remains in place to support the finished bookmark.

You will need

Masking tape

6 x 8 in (15 x 20 cm) clear acetate

½ yd (50 cm) x ½ in (12 mm) white cotton tape

DMC fil à dentelles 80, 1 skein of each of the following colors:

Lilac (210)

Pale pink (605)

Sugar pink (3609)

Rose pink (3688)

Antique pink (3727)

Sewing thread in pink

Key

DMC fil à dentelles 80

1 Pea stitch in lilac 210

2 Side stitch in antique pink 3727

3 Cloth stitch in sugar pink 3609

4 Double Brussels in rose pink 3688

5 Single Brussels in pale pink 605

Preparing the outline

1 Trace or photocopy the template below and tape it, right side up, to the acetate.

2 Baste the cotton tape in place around the outline, starting at A. Turn the raw end under and slipstitch it down along the fold line.

3 Machine stitch the tape in place, along the center of its width.

Stitching the design

1 Using fil à dentelles, make the four straight cordonnettes (marked B on the stitch diagram) which divide the sections. Take two long stitches across the gap for each cordonnette and secure in the tape at each side. Couch these stitches down with the same thread, at ⅛ in (3 mm) intervals.

2 Start at the top of the bookmark and work the needlelace, following the stitch diagram and key.

3 Work plain cordonnettes to cover the straight dividing stitches (page 75).

4 Trim the acetate close to the machine stitching so that the edges are hidden behind the tape.

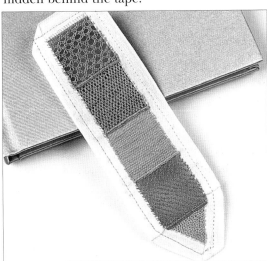

Needlelace bookmark template and stitch diagram: actual size

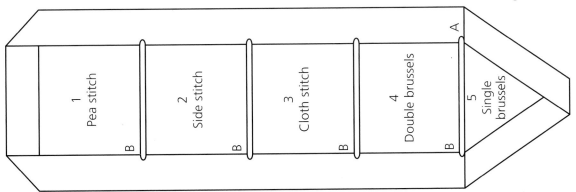

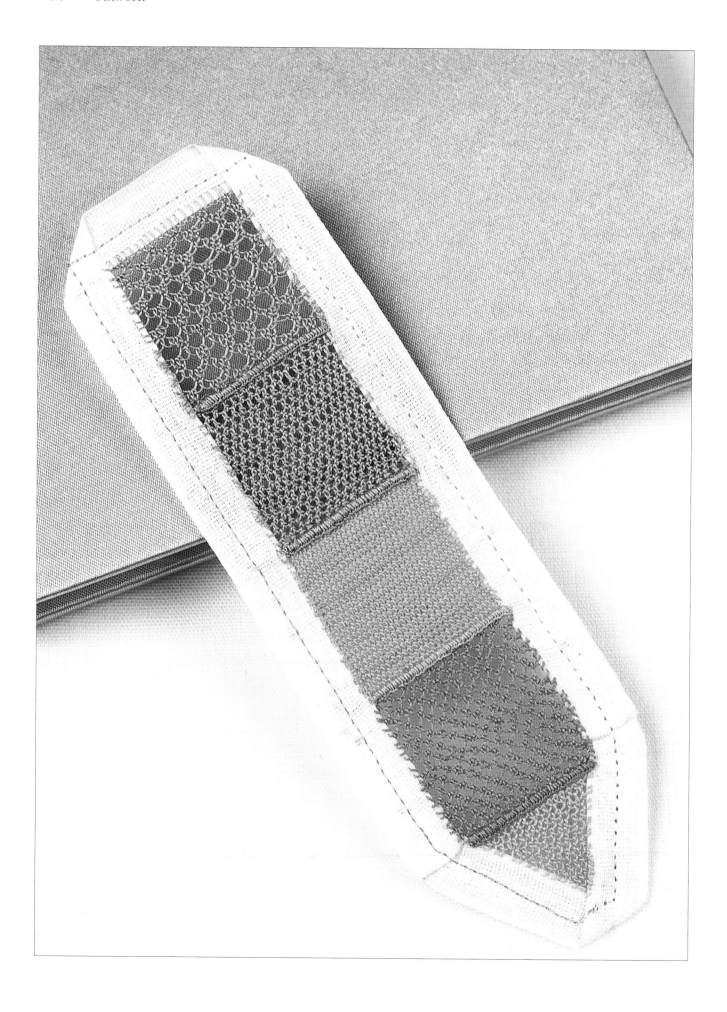

Smocking

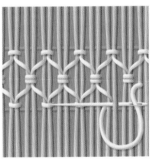

Smocking

Smocking is a form of embroidery made on top of pleats. This makes the work elastic and controls the fullness of the fabric in a decorative way, making it highly suitable for children's clothing. The choices of fabric, stitch design, color and texture make each smocked creation a unique work of art.

FABRICS

Cotton is lovely for summer wear and for winter, fabrics of brushed cotton, wool and cotton blends, fine pinwale corduroy and lightweight velvet can be used. Silk offers a luxurious feel for special occasions, but busy mothers with little time for ironing may prefer a drip-dry polyester cotton.

THREADS

Stranded embroidery floss is the most popular thread used. The six strands can be separated so that the appropriate number of strands can be used for a particular weight of fabric. Coton à broder is a single-ply twisted thread, which some people find easier to handle. Stranded silk is the thread of choice when working with silk fabric. Metallic thread can give a dramatic effect, but is not easy to handle and the type with an inner core should be avoided as the core is exposed with repeated stitching. Stranded metallic thread works best, but you must draw the thread through the fabric rather than pull the needle to keep the thread from wearing on the eye of the needle. The length of thread required for smocking depends on the stitch chosen. You will also need strong gathering thread in a contrasting color to the fabric to gather the pleats.

NEEDLES

Use sharp-pointed embroidery or crewel needles. Sizes 5 to 8 are generally used for smocking. The shaft of the needle should correspond to the size of the thread so that the hole produced is large enough for the thread to pass through, which reduces the wear on the thread. Size 7 embroidery is the most commonly used size for three to four strands of embroidery floss.

SMOCKING TRANSFER DOTS

The dots are printed in silver, yellow or blue on sheets of fine tissue paper. They are easily washed out of the fabric, so select the color to contrast with the fabric so that you can see the dots easily while working. Sheets are available for different spacings of dots to suit different fabrics and are graded alphabetically, although the widest choice is available in silver. For example, the spacings on size A sheets are ⅜ x ⅜ in (8 x 9 mm) where the first measurement indicates the distance between dots across the sheet and therefore the depth of the pleat, and the second measurement indicates the distance between each row of dots. Size A gives deeper pleats and is suitable for heavier fabrics, whereas size K, with ³⁄₁₆ x ³⁄₁₆ in (4 x 4 mm) suits finer fabrics.

OTHER EQUIPMENT

You can produce a similar grid of dots on the wrong side of the fabric using a ruler and a transfer pencil or water-erasable pen.
Special hand-operated smocking pleaters, which produce perfect pleats in minutes, are also available.

USES

Smocking's quality of slight stretchiness makes it ideal for children's wear, allowing a garment to give with the child's movements. It also has many other decorative applications in embellishing furnishing accessories, such as cushions and curtain headings, Christmas decorations and gifts.

Preparing the fabric

Iron the fabric so that it is smooth, ready for gathering. Cut the required length for the smocking project. It is important that the fabric is cut on the grain to ensure that the pleats fall correctly. Some fabric can be torn to establish the grain, but for more delicate fabric a thread should be drawn from one selvage to the other, to provide a cutting line.

To decide on the width of fabric: Always work a small sample of the same fabric first to assist your calculations. Fabric thickness: fine voile, cotton lawn and silk may require four to five times the finished width; medium-weight cotton may require two and a half times, and thick fabric, such as velvet or fine corduroy, may need twice the finished width. Spacing of smocking dots: the wider the dots are spaced, the more fabric is needed.

Choice of stitch: some are more elastic than others; those such as cable, rope and stem stitches, which go straight along a gathering line are less stretchy than those, such as wave stitch, worked between two gathering lines.

To transfer the dots: Cut off the number of rows required for the project. Pin the strip, with the raised transfer surface face down, to the wrong side of the fabric, making sure that the rows run straight with the grain. Heat the iron to a temperature suitable for the fabric and following the transfer manufacturer's instructions. With one single firm sweep, iron the dots onto the fabric. Do not repeat the action as this may cause smudging. Peel off the transfer paper and throw it away as it cannot be reused.

To pleat the fabric: Thread a needle with a length of strong, contrasting gathering thread about 4 in (10 cm) longer than the width of the fabric and firmly knot the end. Work on the wrong side, start with a back stitch and then pick up each dot on the first row, taking the needle in on one side and out the other side of each dot. When the row is complete, unthread the needle and leave the loose thread. Repeat for successive rows.

When all the rows have been picked up, gather the fabric to the correct width. Secure the threads by tying them in pairs or by wrapping pairs around a pin in a figure eight. As a rough guide for traditional smocking, the appropriate width is between 10 and 15 percent less than the width required for the finished garment, depending on the chosen stitch and the tension. When the smocking is complete, the gathering threads are pulled out and the work eases out by 10 to 15 percent. Form the gathers into neat vertical pleats by stroking them with the blunt end of a needle.

Fabrics with regular dots, checks and striped patterns can be gathered without transferring dots, but work a sample first to assess the amount of width reduction. If the fabric has dots, pick them up in the same way as with transfers. If the fabric has stripes, draw parallel lines across the fabric.

Starting and finishing

Right-handed stitchers generally work from left to right and left-handed from right to left. The stitch instructions are give for a right-handed stitcher, but can easily be reversed for left-handed stitching. For each stitch, pick up the top third of the pleat. If too much fabric is picked up, the elasticity of the finished work is reduced.

To start Knot the end of the thread. Bring the needle up to the right side of the fabric in the valley between the first and second pleat, a needle's width above or below the gathering thread, depending on the chosen stitch. It should be so close that once the stitch is in place, it touches the gathering line. Make a stitch, placing the needle into the pleat horizontally and working towards the start of the row.

To finish Take the needle down into the valley behind the last pleat. The needle comes out on top of a pleat on the wrong side. Secure the thread with small stitches on top of the pleat, making a loop and taking the needle through the loop twice to form a knot. Try to finish a thread under a bar stitch, whether at the end of a row or in the middle.

It is not advisable to use very long lengths of thread, which would become worn. Simply finish off as described above. To start a new thread, bring the needle up in the same valley behind the last stitch worked.

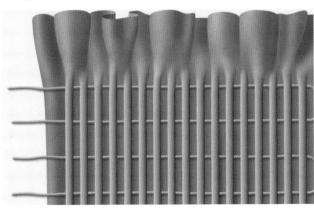

Picking up the dots with gathering thread   Pulling up the gathers evenly

How to make smocking stitches

Stem Stitch

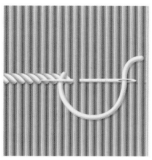

1 Cut a length of thread about three and a half times the length of the row. Bring the needle up just above the gathering line, on the left

side of the first pleat. With the thread lying below the gathering line, pick up the second pleat on the same line from right to left to make a horizontal bar stitch. The stitch looks angled although the needle is inserted horizontally. Pull the thread through until it comes to rest, ending with a gentle tug, but without distorting the pleat. Continue in this way to complete the row.

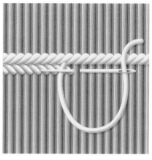

2 When stem stitch is worked directly below a line of rope stitch, a herringbone pattern is produced.

Cable Stitch

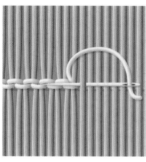

Cut a length of thread about three and a half times the length of the row. Bring the

needle up just above the gathering line, on the left side of the first pleat. With

the thread lying below the gathering line, pick up the second pleat on the same line from right to left to make a horizontal stitch. Pull the thread through until it comes to rest, ending with a gentle tug, but without distorting the pleat, to complete a "down" cable stitch.
For the next stitch, make

sure the thread lies above the gathering line. Make a stitch in the next pleat as before to complete an "up" cable stitch.
Continue, alternating the thread position for successive stitches to create the cable pattern to the end of the row.

Double Cable Stitch

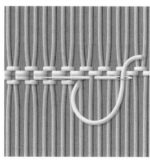

Work a second row of cable stitch immediately below the first, starting with an up cable stitch to make a mirror-imaged pattern. This produces a linked-chain effect.

Rope Stitch (also known as Outline Stitch)

Cut a length of thread about three and a half times the length of the row. Bring the needle up just above the gathering line, on the left side of the first pleat. With the thread lying above the gathering line, pick up the second pleat on the same

line from right to left to make a horizontal stitch. Pull the thread through until it comes to rest, ending with a gentle tug, but without distorting the pleat.
Continue in the same way to complete the row.

Chevron Stitch

Work this stitch on two gathering lines. Cut a length of thread about four and a half times the length of the row. Bring the needle up just above the lower line on the left side of the first pleat.

With the thread lying below the gathering line, pick up the second pleat on the same line from right to left to make a horizontal bar stitch. Pull the thread through until it comes to

rest, ending with a gentle tug, but without distorting the pleat, to complete a bar stitch.

With the thread lying below, pick up the next pleat from right to left just below the top gathering line and make a stitch inserting the needle horizontally. Pull the thread through, as before.

With the thread lying above the gathering line, work a horizontal bar stitch at the same level as the previous stitch, just below the

gathering line.

With the thread lying above, pick up the next pleat from right to left just above the bottom gathering line to make a downward stitch inserting the needle horizontally.

With the thread lying below the gathering line, complete the sequence with a bar stitch over the next stitch. Repeat this sequence to the end of the row.

Half-space Chevron Stitch (also known as Baby Wave Stitch)

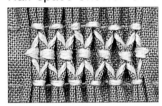

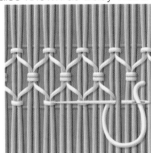

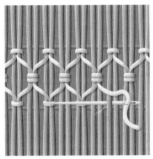

1 This half-size version of chevron stitch allows two mirror-imaged rows to be

worked in the same space. Work the first row in the same way as for chevron stitch, but so that it occupies only half the distance between gathering rows. Make the stitches just within the halfway line because the thread takes up space and you must allow space for the second row.

2 Work a second row of chevron stitch as a mirror image immediately below the first.

Wave Stitch (also known as Trellis Stitch)

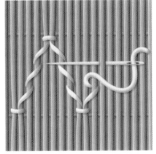

This stitch looks like an extended chevron stitch. The angle of each line in the wave depends on how many extra stitches, or steps, there are between the bar stitches. This method is for three steps. Work this stitch on two gathering lines and cut a length of thread about four

times the length of the row. Bring the needle up just above the lower line on the left side of the first pleat. With the thread lying below the gathering line, pick up the second pleat on the same line from right to left to make a horizontal bar stitch. Pull the thread

through until it comes to rest, ending with a gentle tug, but without distorting the pleat.

With the thread lying below, pick up the next pleat from right to left to make a horizontal stitch a third of the distance towards the top gathering line to make the first step. Make the second step in the next pleat in the same way another third of the distance on. Make the third step in the same way just below the top gathering line. Although the steps appear to be angled, horizontal stitches must be

worked. Pull the thread through, as before.

With the thread lying above the gathering line, work a horizontal bar stitch over the next pleat, just below the gathering line.

With the thread lying above, reverse the sequence to make a downward wave, finishing with a bar stitch. Repeat the wave pattern to the end of the row, remembering that as you work up the wave, the thread must lie below the stitch line and vice versa as you work down.

Wave Diamonds

Work a second row of wave stitch immediately below the first to make a mirror image and produce a diamond effect. The stitches in the middle of the diamond are "surface honeycomb diamonds" (see opposite).

Surface Honeycomb Stitch

This stitch is similar to chevron stitch except that the upward and downward stitches are not worked on a new pleat. It uses a lot of thread. If the thread runs out, see page 141.

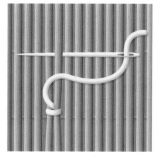

1 Work this stitch on two gathering lines and cut a long length of thread. Bring the needle up just above the lower line on the left side of the first pleat. With the thread lying below the

gathering line, pick up the second pleat on the same line from right to left to make a horizontal bar stitch. Pull the thread through between the two pleats until it comes to rest, ending with a gentle tug, but without distorting the pleat. With the thread lying below the gathering line, pick up the second pleat from right to left just below the top gathering line to make an upward stitch.

2 With the thread lying above the top gathering line, pick up the next pleat from right to left to make a horizontal bar stitch just below the line.

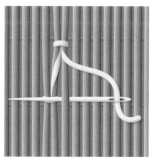

3 With the thread up, pick up the same pleat from right to left, just above the bottom gathering line.

4 With the thread lying below the bottom gathering line, pick up the next pleat on the same line from right to left to make a horizontal bar.

5 Continue, repeating the same sequence to the end of the row.

Surface Honeycomb Diamonds

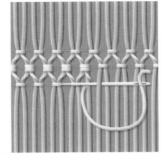

Work a second row of surface honeycomb stitch immediately below the first to make a mirror image and produce a diamond effect. The diamonds can be worked individually as shown in the photograph.

Honeycomb Stitch

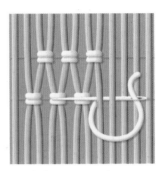

This is usually worked in a thread to match the color of the fabric so that the main focus is on the way the fabric is manipulated in a diamond pattern. It uses a lot of thread. If the thread runs out, see page 141.
1 Work this stitch on two gathering lines. Bring the needle up just below the lower line on the left side of the first pleat.
With the thread lying below

the gathering line, pick up the second and first pleats from right to left to make a bar stitch next to the starting point and just above the gathering line. Pull the thread through, ending with a gentle tug, but without distorting the pleat.
With the thread lying below the gathering line, insert the needle into the right side of the second pleat again, next to the previous stitch. Slide

the needle up behind the second pleat, bringing it out above the top gathering line on the left of the second pleat.
With the thread lying above the gathering line, pick up the second and third pleats from right to left and make a bar stitch as before above the gathering line.
2 With the thread lying above the gathering line, insert the needle into the

third pleat next to the previous stitch. Slide it down behind the pleat, bringing it out just below the bottom gathering line on the left of the fourth pleat.
Repeat these two stitches to the end of the row.
3 To create the diamond pattern, repeat the honeycomb stitch on the next two rows.

Vandyke Stitch

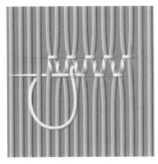

This stitch offers plenty of elasticity and, unusually, is worked from right to left. It uses a lot of thread. If the thread runs out, see page 141.
Work this stitch on two

gathering lines and cut a long length of thread. Bring the needle up just below the top gathering line between the first and second pleats. Make an invisible horizontal stitch from right to left on

the second pleat.
With the thread lying above the gathering line, pick up the first and second pleats from right to left to make a bar stitch next to the start point.
With the thread lying above the gathering line, pick up the second and third pleats from right to left just above the bottom gathering line. Pull the thread through with a gentle tug.
With the thread lying below the gathering line, pick up

the second and third pleats from right to left to make a bar stitch.
With the thread lying below the gathering line, pick up the third and fourth pleats from right to left just below the top gathering line.
With the thread lying above the gathering line, pick up the third and fourth pleats from right to left to make a bar stitch. Continue in the same sequence to the end of the row.

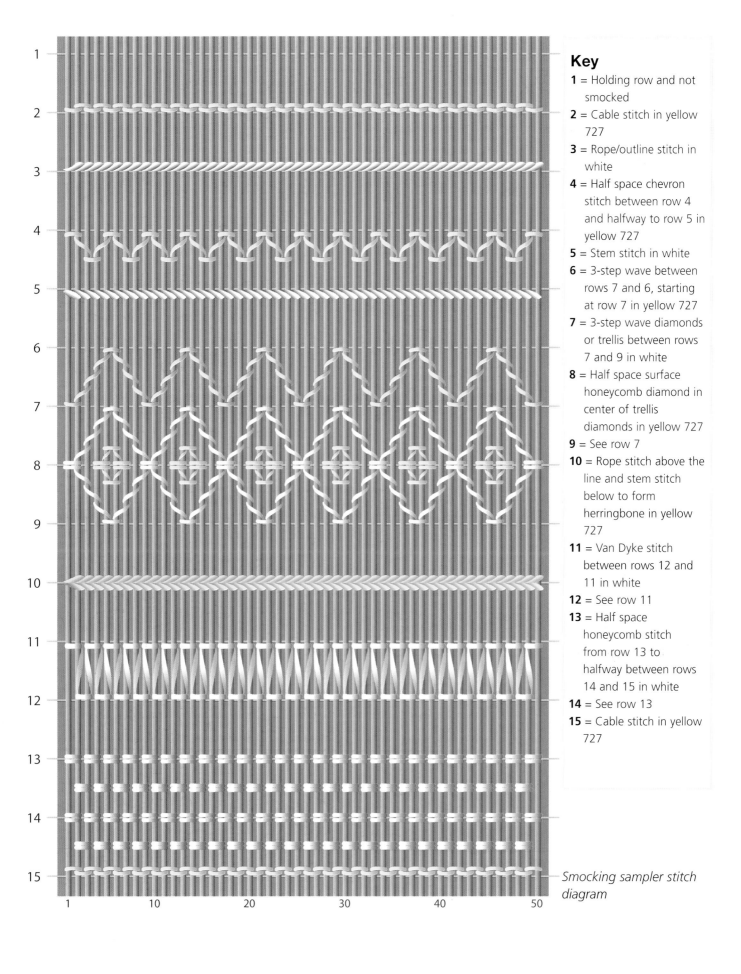

Key

1 = Holding row and not smocked

2 = Cable stitch in yellow 727

3 = Rope/outline stitch in white

4 = Half space chevron stitch between row 4 and halfway to row 5 in yellow 727

5 = Stem stitch in white

6 = 3-step wave between rows 7 and 6, starting at row 7 in yellow 727

7 = 3-step wave diamonds or trellis between rows 7 and 9 in white

8 = Half space surface honeycomb diamond in center of trellis diamonds in yellow 727

9 = See row 7

10 = Rope stitch above the line and stem stitch below to form herringbone in yellow 727

11 = Van Dyke stitch between rows 12 and 11 in white

12 = See row 11

13 = Half space honeycomb stitch from row 13 to halfway between rows 14 and 15 in white

14 = See row 13

15 = Cable stitch in yellow 727

Smocking sampler stitch diagram

How to Stitch the Smocking Sampler

A small sampler worked in stranded embroidery floss, to practice and display a range of smocking stitches. As with a panel worked on a garment, there is a holding row at top and bottom.

You will need

Size H smocking transfer dots
16 in x 7 in (40 x 17.5 cm) firm cotton
    fabric
Size 7 crewel needle
Strong gathering thread in a contrasting
    color to the fabric
Smocking pleater (optional)
DMC stranded embroidery floss, one
    skein each of the following colors:
White (blanc)
Yellow (727)
4½ x 7 in (12.5 x 17.5 cm) cardboard
Masking tape
Frame and mat with 3½ x 5½ in
    (9 x 14 cm) window
Pins

Preparing the fabric

1 Read through all the instructions carefully before starting. Cut a 13 in (32 cm) strip of transfer dots with 16 gathering rows and find the centre of the strip. Find the center of the strip of fabric.
2 Place the transfer strip on the wrong side of the fabric, matching both center lines so that there is a 1½ in (4 cm) border of fabric at each end of the transfer strip. Iron the dots onto the fabric.
3 Pick up the dots using the gathering thread. Check that you have the 50 pleats needed to complete the pattern. If you are using a smocking pleater, gather 16 rows spaced ½ in (1 cm) apart and release the gathers at one end for the 1½ in (4 cm) border. Count 50 pleats and release remaining pleats.
4 Tie off the gathering threads of rows 2–15 in pairs so that the width across the pleats is 3 in (7.5 cm). The top and bottom gathering rows hold the pleats neatly in vertical alignment above and below the smocking. They are not smocked, but are left in place to make mounting easier. Tie them off to give a width of 3½ in (9 cm).

Stitching the design

1 Use three strands of embroidery floss for each row of smocking. Separate the strands individually and then realign them.
2 Follow the stitch diagram row by row.

Mounting the smocking

1 When the smocking is complete, remove the gathering threads from rows 2 to 15.
2 Attach the sampler to the backing board with masking tape, turning over the borders and positioning it so that it will appear in the window of the mat.
3 Place the mat over the sampler and insert it into the frame.

Blocking the smocking

1 If the smocking is for a garment, the work must be blocked to the required finished width. Remove the gathering threads, but leave the holding rows in place.
2 Pin the work to a padded board and ease out the pleats to the required width.
3 Steam the smocking, either by passing a steam iron just above the stitched area, by spraying the work with a water atomizer and using a normal iron in the same way, or by applying heat with a hair dryer. Do not touch the pleats with the iron or the dryer.
4 Leave the pins in place until the work is thoroughly dry and then remove the pins. The smocked work is now ready to incorporate into the garment.

Canvas Work

Needlepoint

Needlepoint is an extremely popular form of needlework that is stitched on canvas, often following a chart or working over a screen-printed image. It is sometimes known as tapestry because the finished result looks very similar to a woven tapestry. Many traditional and modern designs have been influenced by the scenes depicted in such tapestries. Needlepoint designs can be worked solely in tent stitch or in half cross stitch to produce realistic and intricate images. However, there are also many other stitches, both slanting and straight, that can be used to great effect, either on their own or in combinations. The wide range of shades available in needlepoint yarn enables stitchers to create richly colored designs that will last a lifetime.

CANVAS
There are various types of canvas on which needlepoint stitches can be worked and they are all available in a variety of mesh sizes, with 10 and 12 gauge being the most popular. Canvas is normally available in a natural tan color and white. Plain single canvas consists of single threads woven under and over each other. Double canvas has pairs of threads in the same weave and is useful because it can be used for both gros point stitching and finer petit point. Interlocked canvas, with threads that lock together at each intersection, provides a very stable base for diagonal stitches, which would otherwise be prone to distort the canvas.

THREADS
Pure wool yarn is most commonly used for needlepoint work – it covers the canvas well and provides a strong and durable finish. Persian wool consists of three individual strands of two-ply yarn. The strands can be separated, enabling the stitcher to work finer stitches with just one or two of the strands. Tapestry wool is a single-stranded, four-ply yarn, and crewel wool is a single-stranded, two-ply yarn. Pearl cotton, or coton perlé can also be used for more decorative pieces. Always work with relatively short lengths to prevent the yarn from wearing thin with repeated pulling through the holes in the canvas. Thin yarn will not cover the canvas properly, which will then be visible through the stitching.

NEEDLES
Use blunt-ended tapestry needles. They are available in a variety of sizes, so choose one with an eye that accommodates your chosen yarn and passes easily through the holes of the canvas.

USES
Needlepoint is very popular for scatter cushion covers, and small pieces of furniture, such as firescreens, curtain tiebacks and footstools, because it wears well. Larger pieces of needlepoint for upholstering chairs, for example, make a more ambitious project but give stunning results.

Preparing the canvas

Cut a piece of canvas that is at least 4 in (10 cm) bigger than the final stitched area. Bind the edges with masking tape to prevent yarn from catching on them and wearing thin (pilling).

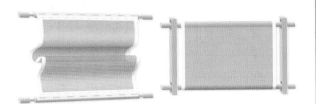

Mounting the canvas in an embroidery frame

Binding the canvas edge with masking tape

You will find the canvas much easier to work with if it is mounted in an embroidery frame. The most common of these is a roller frame, which allows you to roll the canvas up and down to reveal the next area to be worked. It will also keep the canvas taut and prevent it from distorting.

Starting and finishing

To start small, compact needlepoint stitches, simply leave a short end on the wrong side. Work over the end with the first few stitches so that it is held securely in place. To finish off, pass the needle and thread back through a few stitches of the same color on the reverse side of the work.

When working larger stitches, it may not always be possible to anchor a loose end at the very beginning. For these stitches, tie a knot in the end of the yarn and take the needle through the canvas from the right side a short distance from where the stitching is to begin and outside the stitching area, leaving the knot on the top. When the stitching is complete, snip off the knot carefully and sew the end into a matching area on the wrong side.

How to make needlepoint stitches

Tent Stitch (also known as Petit Point and Continental Tent Stitch)

This is the most commonly used needlepoint stitch. It is small, neat and can be used to create intricate patterns and fine details, especially on double canvas. The stitch produces a diagonal effect on both sides of the canvas and therefore is prone to distortion. Work the stitch over one canvas intersection and start new stitches in the hole next to the previous starting point.

Half Cross Stitch

When finished, half cross stitch looks like tent stitch (above). However, it produces a straight bar on the wrong side of the fabric making it less prone to distortion.

Brick Stitch

Brick stitch is a type of back stitch (page 12) that can be worked both horizontally and vertically. Start with a foundation row of alternating long and short straight stitches, working the long stitches over three

canvas threads and the short ones over two. Work all subsequent rows over three canvas threads so that the stitches interlock just like bricks. Finish with a final row of long and short stitches.

Parisian Stitch

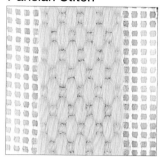

The neat effect created by this stitch is made up of rows of upright stitches. Work alternate stitches over one and then three horizontal canvas threads.

On subsequent rows, reverse the order so that the long stitches fit neatly into the spaces created by the short stitches in the row below.

Long and Short Stitch

This has a similar appearance to Brick Stitch, but the stitches are generally worked over more canvas threads. It is perfect for shading in several tones of one color. Start with a foundation row of alternating straight long and short stitches, working

the long stitches over, for example, four canvas threads and the short ones over two. Work all subsequent rows over four canvas threads so that the stitches interlock. Finish with a final row of long and short stitches.

Hungarian Stitch

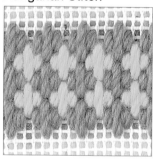

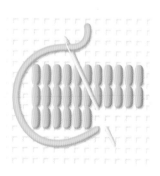

This stitch produces a neat pattern that can be worked in one color or in contrasting stripes. Work the three upright stitches for each little block in the pattern over two, four and then two horizontal canvas threads. Then start the next block

after two vertical threads. On the next row make sure that the longest stitches go into the holes between the blocks of the first row, so that the rows are set into each other.

Straight Gobelin Stitch

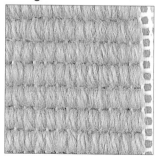

This is the most basic of straight stitches and makes a simple filling stitch that quickly covers large areas of canvas. Work it from bottom to top over two canvas threads.

Gobelin Stitch (also known as Slanted Gobelin Stitch and Gros Point)

To achieve the correct tension, Gobelin stitch must always be worked as shown in the diagram. Whether working from left to right or from right to left, take the needle down at the bottom and bring it up at the top of the stitch.

Encroaching Gobelin Stitch

This stitch is made up of close rows, each overlapping the previous one by one thread. Work each stitch over five horizontal threads and one vertical thread, longer than regular Gobelin stitch.

Mosaic Stitch

 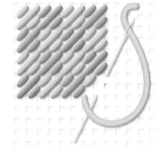

Mosaic stitch is like Hungarian stitch, but worked diagonally, with the blocks right next to each other. It produces a small checkerboard pattern that may be worked in one or more colors. Work the three diagonal stitches for each little block over one, two and then one canvas intersection.

Checker Stitch

 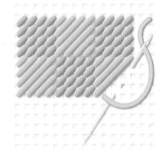

This stitch can be worked all in one color or in two tones of the same color to create a checkerboard effect. All the squares of the pattern are worked over four horizontal and four vertical canvas threads. Work 16 small diagonal stitches, over one canvas intersection each, for alternate squares and seven larger stitches, graduating in length, for the remaining squares.

Scottish Stitch

This interestingly textured stitch is worked in two parts. First work a row of small diagonal stitches. For each square, make the stitches over one, two, three, two and then one canvas intersection with one vertical

canvas thread between each square. Then fill in the lines between the squares with small diagonal stitches over one canvas thread. Add a border in the same small stitches.

Cashmere Stitch

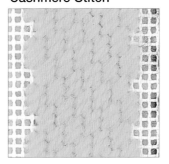

This is another stitch that produces a woven effect. Work the pattern diagonally, first making one short stitch worked over one canvas thread, then two longer stitches both worked over

two horizontal and two vertical threads. On subsequent rows, the stitches sit neatly alongside each other. Finish each row with a final stitch over one thread.

Diagonal Stitch

The diagonal rows created by this stitch run from top left to bottom right. Work the satin stitches in each row in a continuing sequence over two, three, four and then three horizontal and vertical

canvas threads. Finish each row with a final stitch over two threads. The longest stitches in each row fit neatly inside the shortest ones in the previous row.

Milanese Stitch

Milanese stitch is made up of small triangles created in four rows of diagonal backstitch. On the first row, work the stitches alternately over one and then four canvas intersections. Work

alternately over two and three intersections for the second row and over three and two intersections for the third. Work over four and one intersections for the final row.

Byzantine Stitch

This stitch quickly covers the canvas and produces the effect of woven fabric. It can be worked in one color or in contrasting bands. Work five long diagonal satin stitches over four vertical and four

horizontal canvas threads, going up the canvas. Then work five similar stitches across the canvas. Repeat this sequence to complete a diagonal row.

Jacquard Stitch

This stitch produces a similar stepped effect to Byzantine stitch, but here rows of stitches of different lengths alternate. For the first row, work five diagonal satin stitches over two vertical and two horizontal canvas

threads, going up the canvas. Then work five similar stitches across the canvas. Repeat this sequence to complete a diagonal row. Work the second row with small stitches over just one intersection.

Fishbone Stitch

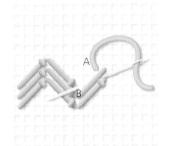

First work one long diagonal stitch over three horizontal and three vertical canvas threads. Bring the needle up at A, then work a small diagonal stitch in the opposite direction over one

intersection at the end of the long stitch. Bring the needle back up at B. Continue, repeating this combination to make the stitches along alternate diagonals.

Linen Stitch

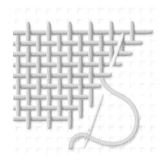

Worked in diagonal rows from left to right, linen stitch forms a compact pattern with a woven appearance. Starting at the bottom, work a row of straight horizontal stitches, each one over two vertical canvas threads and one thread to the right of the

previous one. Now start at the bottom again and work a row of straight vertical stitches, over two horizontal canvas threads, to cover the ends of the horizontal stitches. As you work, be careful not to split the yarn in previous stitches.

Upright Cross Stitch
(also known as St George Stitch)

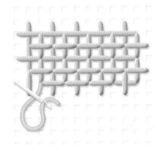

This stitch can be used both as a border stitch and as a textured filling stitch. It can be worked over any number of threads, but for good

coverage of the canvas, it should be worked over two vertical and two horizontal threads.

Double Cross Stitch
(also known as Leviathan Stitch and Smyrna Stitch)

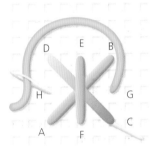

A variation of cross stitch, this stitch creates an unusual textured finish. First work a large cross stitch over four horizontal and four vertical canvas threads working in

the sequence A to D. Then bring the needle up at E and work a large upright cross stitch over the top working in the sequence E to H.

Broad Diagonal Cross Stitch

This is a bold stitch that is useful for covering large areas of canvas. First work three long parallel diagonal stitches, one above the other, working each over five intersections from top left to bottom right. Then bring the needle up three holes above

the last stitch and work another three parallel diagonal stitches in the same way, but in the opposite direction to cover the first three.

Cushion Stitch

1 This stitch is worked over six horizontal and six vertical canvas threads. First make 11 diagonal stitches, graduating in length, to fill the block.
2 Then make six diagonal stitches in the opposite direction to cover half of the original block.

Algerian Eye Stitch

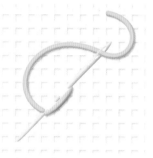

threads and then work another stitch through the same holes.
2 Continue around the block in the same way. As you work each stitch twice into the same hole, pull them as tight as the canvas will allow.

1 This stitch can be used individually to produce small star-shaped blocks or repeated to create a pretty pattern. Make the first stitch diagonally over two canvas

Diamond Eyelet Stitch

Diamond eyelet stitch is worked in a similar way to Algerian eye stitch in that all the individual stitches share a common central hole, but the stitches form a diamond shape. Start by making the top straight stitch over three horizontal canvas threads

and work around the shape clockwise.

Rice Stitch (also known as Crossed Corners Stitch)

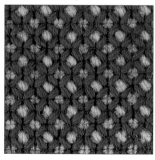
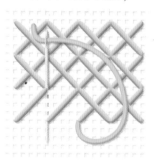

1 This stitch creates an unusual pattern when worked in two contrasting colors. Use one color to work rows of large cross stitches over four vertical and four horizontal threads.
2 Use a second color to work small diagonal stitches over each end of the original cross stitches. The small stitches also meet and look like cross stitches.

Rhodes Stitch

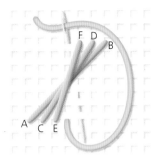

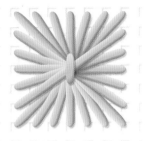

1 Beginning at the bottom left of the square, make a diagonal stitch over six canvas intersections from A to B. Bring the needle back up one hole to the right of A, at C, and make a stitch into the hole one vertical thread to the left of B, at D. Come up again at E and continue to work all around the square.

2 A small vertical stitch worked over two threads through all the layers can be added if desired.

Herringbone Stitch

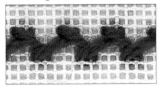

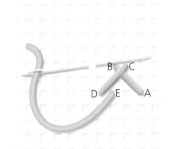

Bring the needle up at A and take it back down at B. Then bring the needle up at C and take it back down at D. Bring the needle up at E ready to start the next stitch.

Norwich Stitch

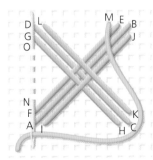

1 Start by making a large cross stitch across nine canvas intersections from A to B and C to D. Bring the needle up one canvas thread to the left of the top right of the original cross, at E and make a diagonal stitch down to one thread above the

bottom left of the original, at F. Now bring the needle up at G and make a diagonal stitch down to H. Bring the needle up again at I and make a diagonal stitch up to J. Complete the first round by bringing the needle up at K and down at L.

2 Continue in the same way around the entire square.

Long-legged Cross Stitch

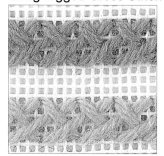

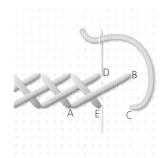

This is a perfect stitch for borders. First work a long diagonal stitch over seven vertical and four horizontal threads from A to B. Bring the needle back up four threads directly below, at C and make the next stitch backwards over four vertical and four horizontal threads, taking the needle down at D. Then bring the needle back up four threads directly below, at E to start the next stitch. All subsequent stitches are worked into common holes.

Knotted Stitch

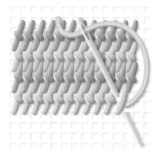

This produces a very dense, strong stitch with each row encroaching on the previous one by one thread. First make a long stitch over one vertical and three horizontal canvas threads. Then make a short stitch over the central intersection of the long stitch. In the second row, make sure the tops of the long stitches occupy the same hole as the bottom of the short stitches.

Velvet Stitch (also known as Plush Stitch)

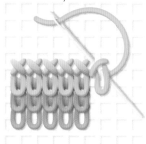

This looks like the pile on a carpet and the loops can be cut and trimmed to length if required. Work a diagonal stitch from left to right over one canvas intersection and bring the needle back out in the bottom left hole again. Take the needle back into the top right hole, but leave a loop of thread of the required length. Bring the needle out one hole below the top right hole and make a diagonal stitch over one intersection to complete the cross. Bring the needle out of the previous hole again to begin the next stitch. For fine yarns, work the rows directly above one another and for thicker yarn, increase the spacing.

Blue-bordered sampler chart, enlarge on a photocopier for ease of working

Blue-bordered sampler key

A Byzantine stitch in turquoise 7037 and blue 7796

B Checker stitch in pale pink 7605 and bright pink 7603

C Double cross stitch in purple 7017

D Cashmere stitch in yellow 7435

E Brick stitch in red 7606 and orange 7740

F Milanese stitch in pale green 7958

G Hungarian stitch in green 7341 and yellow 7435

H Gobelin stitch in blue 7796

I Broad diagonal cross stitch in deep pink 7135

J Straight gobelin stitch in pale green 7958

K Jacquard stitch in red 7606 and yellow 7435

L Algerian eye stitch in red 7606

M Long and short stitch in purple 7017, pale pink 7605, bright pink 7603

N Encroaching gobelin in turquoise 7037

O Mosaic stitch in orange 7740, pale green 7958, yellow 7435, bright pink 7603, blue 7796, turquoise 7037, green 7341, purple 7017

P Long-legged cross stitch in green 7341, pale green 7958

How to Stitch the Needlepoint Samplers

These two colorful samplers will show your stitching skills to perfection. The charts are given to show the general areas in which to work the stitches, but in the true spirit of samplers, they are all interchangeable. Experimentation with the colors will also add to the finished effect.

You will need

15½ x 18½ in (39 x 47 cm) 12-gauge single canvas for each sampler

Masking tape

Tapestry needle

Basting thread

Embroidery frame

For blue-bordered sampler:

DMC tapestry yarn, one skein of each of the following colors:

Purple (7017)

Turquoise (7037)

Deep pink (7135)

Green (7341)

Pale green (7958)

Yellow (7435)

Bright pink (7603)

Pale pink (7605)

Red (7606)

Orange (7740)

Blue (7796)

For green-bordered sampler:

DMC tapestry yarn, one skein of each of the following colors:

Coral (7106)

Pink (7135)

Mid-blue (7314)

Dark blue (7318)

Yellow (7431)

Gold (7436)

Red (7666)

Mauve (7896)

Green (7911)

Preparing the canvas

1 Bind the edges of the canvas (page 6).

2 Mark both center lines on the canvas, each with a row of basting stitches.

3 Mount the canvas on the frame.

4 Mark the center of the chart with a pen.

Stitching the samplers

1 Starting at the center point and following the relevant chart and key, for the blue bordered sampler, begin by working the band of broad diagonal cross stitch that runs across the middle. For the green bordered sampler, start in the center with the area of tent stitch.

2 Continue, following the chart to work the other stitches inside the border in the appropriate colors. Note that some of the stitches use more than one color. Where several colors are used, refer to the picture of the finished design.

3 When all the stitch blocks are complete, add the border in herringbone stitch for the blue-bordered sampler or in upright cross stitch for the green-bordered sampler. To keep the pattern correct, rotate the canvas as you work each side.

Finishing the samplers

1 Block the canvas (page 8) so that the diagonal stitches do not distort the canvas.

2 Lace the canvas over a piece of hardboard and frame as required.

Green-bordered sampler chart, enlarge on a photocopier for ease of working

Green-bordered sampler key

A Rice stitch in gold 7436 and dark blue 7318

B Parisian stitch in yellow 7431

C Norwich stitch in coral 7106 and red 7666

D Velvet stitch in red 7666

E Scottish stitch in green 7911, mid-blue 7314, gold 7436

F Cushion stitch in mauve 7896

G Diagonal stitch in green 7911 and red 7666

H Tent stitch in dark blue 7318, mid-blue 7314, yellow 7431, coral 7106, red 7666, gold 7436, pink 7135, mauve 7896

I Rhodes stitch in yellow 7431 and gold 7436

J Knotted stitch in mauve 7896

K Half cross stitch in coral 7106, yellow 7431, dark blue 7318, mid blue 7314, pink 7135, mauve 7896

L Diamond eyelet stitch in dark blue 7318

M Fishbone stitch in coral 7106

N Upright cross stitch in green 7911 (border), dark blue 7318 and mid-blue 7314 (rows)

O Linen stitch in red 7666

Bargello

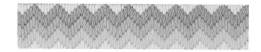

Bargello, or Florentine as it is also called, is all about color and design. It is a deceptively intricate-looking form of needlepoint, worked entirely in straight, upright stitches of varying lengths. However, the design possibilities for Bargello are endless, and once you have mastered the basics, a little bit of experimenting with graph paper and colored pens will lead you into a world of magic. Traditionally, Bargello was worked in three or more shades of one color, with any accents provided by contrasting colors, and shades of blue, pink, green and gold were very popular.

CANVAS

Bargello is worked on traditional single needlepoint canvas. Always mount the canvas in an embroidery frame in order to achieve the correct tension.

THREADS

Pure wool yarn is most commonly used for Bargello – it covers the canvas well and provides a strong and durable finish. Persian wool consists of three individual strands of two-ply yarn. The strands can be separated, enabling the stitcher to work finer stitches with just one or two of the strands. Tapestry wool is a single-stranded, four-ply yarn, and crewel wool is a single-stranded, two-ply yarn.

Always work with relatively short lengths to prevent the yarn from wearing thin with repeated pulling through the holes in the canvas. Thin yarn will not cover the canvas properly, which will then be visible through the stitching.

NEEDLES

Use blunt-ended tapestry needles. They are available in a variety of sizes, so choose one with an eye that accommodates the yarn and passes easily through the holes of the canvas.

OTHER EQUIPMENT

Graph paper and colored pens or pencils are essential for charting the designs.

USES

The finished work is very strong, and since it also covers the canvas quickly, it is ideally suited to large-scale projects such as cushion covers, chair seats and bench cushions.

Working with Bargello charts

Charts usually show just the first, foundation row of the design, which establishes the shape of the pattern. With all Bargello patterns, first work all the whole stitches of your chosen pattern to fill the required area and then work part stitches in the correct color to fill the gaps around the edge.

Preparing the canvas

Cut a piece of canvas that is at least 4 in (10 cm) bigger than the final stitched area. Bind the edges with masking tape to prevent the yarn from catching on them and wearing thin (pilling) (page 151).

You will find the canvas much easier to work with if it is mounted in an embroidery frame (page 151). The most common of these is a roller frame, which allows you to roll the canvas up and down to reveal the next area to be worked. It will also keep the canvas taut and prevent it from distorting.

Starting and finishing

To start small, compact needlepoint stitches, simply leave a short end on the wrong side of the canvas. Work over the end with the first few stitches so that it is held securely in place. To finish off, pass the needle and thread back through a few stitches of the same color on the reverse of the work. When working larger stitches, it may not always be possible to anchor a loose end at the very beginning. For these stitches, tie a knot in the end of the yarn and take the needle through the canvas from the right side a short distance from where the stitching is to begin and outside the stitching area, leaving the knot on the top. When the stitching is complete, snip off the knot and sew the loose end into an appropriate area on the wrong side.

How to make Bargello stitches

Florentine stitch

This simple zigzag stitch is the most basic of all Bargello patterns. Starting with the darkest shade of your chosen color, work a series of straight upright stitches over four canvas threads moving each stitch one thread up or down according to the chart; here each side of the zigzag is made up of five staggered stitches. Work the next row in the next shade, following exactly the same sequence of stitches as in the first row. Continue in the same way, using the shades in succession, to fill the area. To complete the design, work part stitches in the appropriate shades.

Lightning zigzag pattern

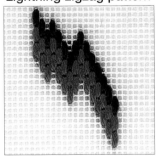 

By varying the number of stitches in each zigzag, more dramatic patterns can be achieved. Each stitch in this lively pattern is worked over three threads and moves up or down by two canvas threads, but there are between three and eight stitches on different parts of the zigzag. The fact that the pattern does not repeat across the row in any way adds to the effect.

Carnation pattern

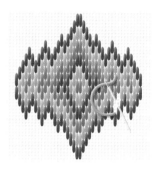

This pattern shows how irregular zigzags can be used to create large motifs. Each stitch is worked over four canvas threads and moves up or down by two canvas threads. Work the darkest color first to give a definite outline for all the other stitches to follow and prevent mistakes. Work the background in the same way, but using just one color.

Curved and arched patterns

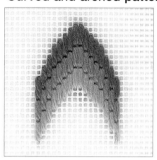

By varying the number of threads that the stitches move up or down, it is possible to create curved and arched patterns. All the stitches are worked over four canvas threads, but at the top of the arch they move by just one horizontal thread each time, whereas at the bottom of the arch they move by two horizontal canvas threads.

Simple repeating borders

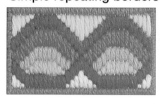

The eyelid motif in the bottom right corner of the sampler is a perfect illustration of the effects that can be achieved by working stitches of varying lengths within a pattern. The top and bottom rows are worked over three canvas threads, and although they establish the boundaries of the design, they do not act as a guide for all other stitches to follow. The space within the outline is filled with rows of stitches that decrease in size as the color shade gets lighter.

Motifs

Individual or repeating motifs are a popular element of Bargello. By working a pair of stitches in each color, a more graphic effect can be achieved as illustrated by this little heart. It is worked in two blocks of color and an outline, with each pair of stitches worked over four canvas threads and moved up or down by two threads.

Four-way Bargello

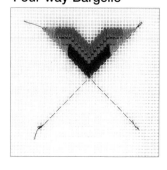

This is one of the most striking patterns. It is worked in four triangular sections, around a center point. First baste two diagonal lines across the area to be stitched. Work the stitches in the top quarter. Turn the canvas clockwise so that you can continue making upright stitches and fill the shape with the same pattern, working stitches along the axis into shared holes. Work the third and fourth quarters in the same way.

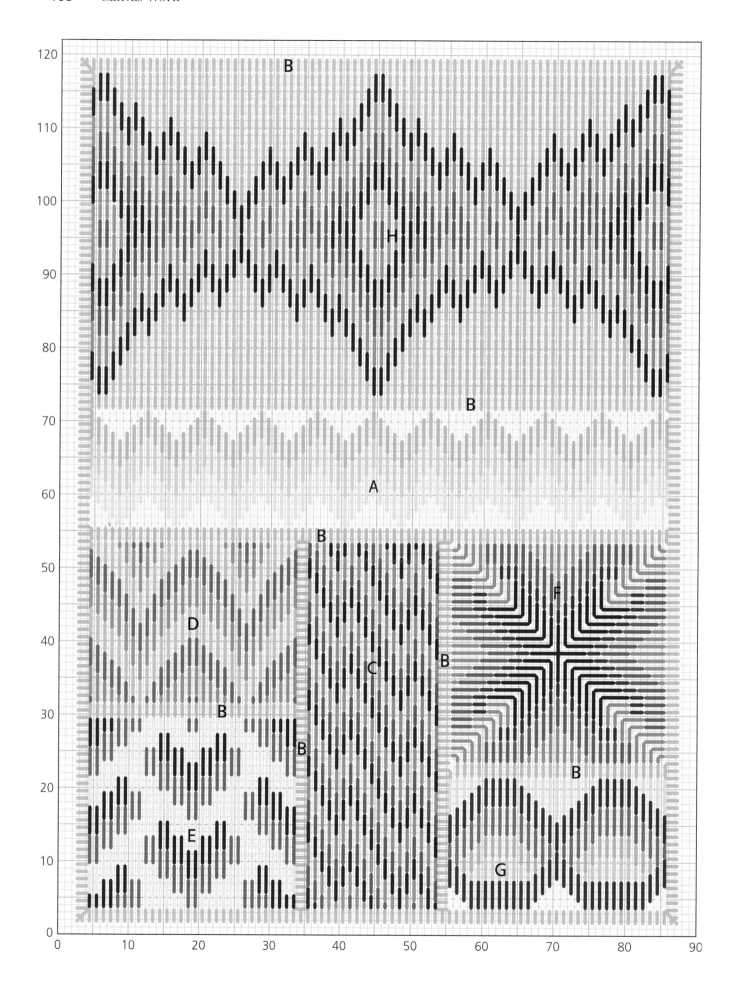

How to Stitch the Bargello Sampler

This unusual sampler combines all the basic elements of Bargello design and makes the perfect practice piece.

You will need

11 x 13½ in (28 x 34 cm) 12-gauge
  single canvas
Embroidery frame
DMC tapestry wool, 1 skein of each of
  the following colors:
Purple (7017)
Turquoise (7037)
Coral (7106)
Mid-blue (7314)
Dark blue (7318)
Bright green (7341)
Pale yellow (7431)
Bright yellow (7435)
Gold (7436)
Dark pink (7603)
Pale pink (7605)
Bright red (7606)
Dark red (7666)
Orange (7740)
Mauve (7896)
Grass green (7911)
Pale green (7958)
Tapestry needle

Bargello sampler chart

Preparing the canvas

1 Bind the edges of the canvas (page 6).
2 Mark both center lines on the canvas, each with a row of basting stitches.
3 Mount the canvas on the frame.
4 Mark the center of the chart with a pen.

Stitching the sampler

1 Following the chart and the key, and starting in the center, work band A in Florentine stitch that runs across the middle of the sampler. Work part stitches in pale yellow above and below the zigzags to complete the band. Now add row B, made of straight stitches in coral over two canvas threads above and below band A.
2 Follow the chart and the key to work the lightning zigzag pattern in block C, with a row B on each side of it. Work the arched pattern in block D, followed by a row of B underneath. Then work the repeated heart motif in block E.
3 Block F is filled with four-way Florentine. You may find it helpful to mark the diagonal center of this area with basting stitches. Start with the top quarter and rotate the canvas for each subsequent quarter. Work a row of B underneath and then fill block G with the eyelid motif.
4 Work the stunning carnation pattern in block H at the top of the sampler to complete the blocks.
5 To complete the sampler, work a fine coral border around all the outer edges as shown on the chart.

Mounting the sampler

1 Place the embroidery right side down on a clean towel and press from the wrong side with a steam iron, gently easing the canvas into its original shape. The canvas does not need blocking as no diagonal stitches, which would distort the canvas, have been used.
2 Lace the canvas over a piece of hardboard (page 8) and frame as required.

Key

A orange 7740, gold 7436, bright yellow 7435 on pale yellow 7431
B coral 7106
C dark blue 7318, turquoise 7037, mid-blue 7314
D grass green 7911, bright green 7341, pale green 7958
E purple 7017, dark pink 7603, pale pink 7605
F purple 7017, mauve 7896, dark red 7666 and grass green 7911
G dark red 7666, bright red 7606, orange 7740, gold 7436 on bright yellow 7435 and
  pale yellow 7431
H dark blue 7318, turquoise 7037 and mid-blue 7314 on pale green 7958

Suppliers

Adrianne's Attic
Tel: 1-866-42-ATTIC
  (1-866-422-8842) for orders
Email: adriannesattic2002@
  yahoo.com
www.adriannes.com
*Online collection of quality imported
and domestic fabrics.*

All Threads
1010 SE 6th St
Lee's Summit, MO 64063
Tel: toll Free: 877-237-5954
e-mail: comment@
  allthreads.com
www.allthreads.com
*Online suppliers of threads for the
home-stitcher.*

Classic Creations
P.O. Box 4204
Crofton
MD 21114
Tel: 301-261-0636
Email: megerstch@aol.com
www.classiccreationssmocking.
  com
*Mail-order supplier of needles and
threads, including metallics and
overdyed.*

Cotton Boll
Village Plaza Mall
99 S. Elliot Road
Chapel Hill
NC 27514
Tel: 919-942-9661
www.thecottonboll.com
*Supplier of natural fibers and hand
sewing products from three stores in
the NC area. Also sewing classes.*

DMC Creative World Ltd
Email: dmcusa@dmc.fr
www.dmc-usa.com
*Online supplier of DMC threads and
needlework products. Products stocked
in stores nationwide.*

Embroidery.com
Tel: 1-800-428-7606
Email: info@embroidery.com
www.embroidery.com
*Online supplier of threads and
embroidery equipment.*

Global Sewing Supply
PO Box 160063
Boiling Springs
SC 29316
Tel: 1-800-948-0287
www.globalsewing.com
*Sewing and craft supplies including
sewing machines and lights. Mail-
order supplier.*

Hancock Fabrics
Head Office
3406 West Main Street
Tupelo
Mississippi 38801
Tel: 1-877-FABRICS
  (1-877-322-7427)
www.hancockfabrics.com
*Large fabric retailer. Stores
nationwide and online supplier.*

Heirlooms Forever
3112 Cliff Gookin Blvd Tupelo
Mississippi 38801
Tel: 662-842-4275
Fax: 662-842-2284
For orders: 800-840-4275
www.sews.com
*Products for all types of stitching.
Online and mail-order supplier.*

Herrschners
2800 Hoover Road
Stevens Point
WI 54492-0001
Tel: 1-800-441-0838 order line
Fax: 1-715-341-2250
Email: customerservice@
  herrschners.com
www.herrschners.com
*Needlework and embroidery threads
and products. Online and mail-order
supplier.*

Hobby Lobby Stores, Inc.
Head Office
7707 S.W. 44th Street
Oklahoma City
OK 73179
www.hobbylobby.com
*General craft and needlework supplier.
Stores nationwide and online supplier
through www.craftsetc.com.*

House of Stitches
1700 Lincolnway Suite 4
LaPorte
IN 46350
Tel: 1-219-326-0544 or
  1-800-455-8517
Email:mail@
  houseofstitches.com
www.houseofstitches.com
*Range of counted cross stitch supplies
and accessories. Online and mail-
order supplier.*

Jo-Ann Fabric and Crafts
Tel: 1-888-739-4120
Email: guest.services@
  jo-annstores.com
www.joann.com
*Large range of fabric and embroidery
products. Stores nationwide and online
supplier.*

Joys Creative Sewing
1032-C 4th Avenue SE
Decatur, AL 35601
Tel: 1-256-351-6196
Fax: 1-256-351-6192
Email: info@
  joyscreativesewing.com
www.joyscreativesewing.com
*Large range of materials for
smocking, embroidery and other
heirloom techniques and embroidery
machines. Mail-order supplier.*

Kathy Neal Company
308 West Hall Street
Thomson, Georgia 30824
Tel: 1-706-595-9696
Email: kathynealco@aol.com
www.kathyneal.net
*Range of needles, fibers and patterns.
Online supplier.*

Madeira USA
Head Office
Madeira USA Headquarters
30 Bayside Court,
Laconia
NH 03246
Tel: 1-800-225-3001
www.madeirausa.com
*Online supplier of Madeira fashion
threads and accessories. Products
stocked in stores nationwide.*

Michaels Stores, Inc.
Head Office
8000 Bent Branch Dr.
Irving
TX 75063
Tel: 1-800-MICHAELS
  (1-800-642-4235)
www.michaels.com
General craft and needlework supplier. Stores nationwide and online supplier.

Needlework Corner
P.O. Box 473
Carbondale
IL 62903-0473
Tel: 1-618-529-5860
www.needleworkcorner.com
Mail order supplier of needlework kits and yarns.

Needlework Plus
Fax: 1-610-705-3039
Email: sales@
  needleworkplus.com
www.needleworkplus.com
Online supplier of a range of stitching products.

Plaid
Tel: 1-800-842-4197
www.plaidonline.com
Online supplier of Plaid needle craft products. Products stocked in stores nationwide.

Quilter's Dream, Inc.
384 Lake Street
Antioch
Illinois 60002
Tel: tollfree (877) 405-7421
Email: dreamquilter@
  ameritech.net
www.quilters-dream.com
Range of fabrics and threads for quilting and embroidery. Mail-order supplier.

The Rag Shop
Head Office
111 Wagaraw Road
Hawthorne, NJ 07506
Tel: 1-973-423-1303
Email:
generalinfo@ragshop.com
www.ragshop.com
Fabric and sewing products and information. Over 60 stores in five states.

The Status Thimble
277 Primrose Road
Burlingame
CA 94010 - 4207
Tel: 1-650-344-1737
Fax : 1-650-344-9126
Email:
info@thestatusthimble.com
www.thestatusthimble.com
This store carries supplies and materials for fine hand needlework. Also a mail-order supplier.

The Stitching Bee, Inc.
240a Main Street
Chatham
NJ 07928
Tel: 1-973-635-6691
Email: stitchbee@aol.com
www.thestitchingbee.com
Range of supplies for all your knitting and needlepoint needs including yarns, patterns, and kits. For mail-order contact the store.

Sulky of America
Head Office
3113 Broadpoint Drive
Punta Gorda
FL 33983
Fax: 941-743-4634
Email: info@sulky.com
www.sulky.com
Sulky threads and products are available in stores nationwide.

Most large department stores carry a good range of fabrics, threads, and accessories. Look in the telephone directory for details of your nearest under Art and Craft Equipment or Needlecraft Retailers.

ASSOCIATIONS

Home Sewing Association
PO Box 1312
Monroeville
PA 15146
Tel: 1-412-372-5950
Fax: 1-412-372-5953
www.sewing.org
This association provides inspiration and education to the home-sewing enthusiast.

The American Sewing Guild
National Headquarters
9660 Hillcroft, Suite 510
Houston, TX 77096
Tel: 713-729-3000
Email: info@asg.org
www.asg.org
This guild provides discounts and news from the sewing industry to stitchers of any skill level.

Index

This edition published in 2006 by
New Holland Publishers (UK) Ltd
London • Cape Town • Sydney • Auckland
www.newhollandpublishers.com

Garfield House, 86-88 Edgware Road, London W2 2EA

80 McKenzie Street, Cape Town 8001, South Africa

Unit 4, 14 Aquatic Drive, Frenchs Forest, NSW 2086, Australia

218 Lake Road, Northcote, Auckland, New Zealand

2 4 6 8 10 9 7 5 3 1

Text, photography and illustrations © 2004 New Holland Publishers (UK) Ltd
Copyright © 2004 New Holland Publishers (UK) Ltd

ISBN 1 84537 203 4

Editor: Karen Hemingway
Design: Sara Kidd
Photographs: Shona Wood
Illustrations: Steve Dew
Editorial Direction: Rosemary Wilkinson

Reproduction by Pica Digital PTE Ltd, Singapore
Printed and bound in Malaysia by
Times Offset (M) Sdn Bhd

NOTE
The measurements for each project are given in imperial and metric. Use only one set of measurements – do not interchange
them because they are not direct equivalents.

ACKNOWLEDGEMENTS
The Publishers would like to thank DMC Creative World Ltd for their kind help in supplying all of the threads
for the stitch samples and projects.